CULTURES OF THE WORLD™
INDONESIA

by Gouri Mirpuri/Robert Cooper

BENCHMARK BOOKS

MARSHALL CAVENDISH
NEW YORK

PICTURE CREDITS
Samsuri Ahmad, APA Photo Library, Archive Photos,
Michele Burgess, Cathay Pacific, Victor Ebenson, Globe
Press, Jill Gocher, HBL Network Photo Agency, Rio Helmi,
Adolf Heuken, Ho Khee Tong, Horizon, Hulton-Deutsch,
Image Bank, Indonesian Archives, Indonesian Embassy of
Singapore, Carl-Bernd Kaehlig, Bjorn Klingwall, Lawrence
Lee, Lawrence Lim, Leonard Lueras, Gouri Mirpuri, Kal
Muller, Christine Osborne Pictures, Photobank, The Straits
Times, Luca Tettoni, Nini Tiley, Tourist Bureau of
Indonesia, Vision Photo Agency, Diane Wilson, Paul Zach

PRECEDING PAGE:
Indonesia has as many dance styles as it has languages and
dialects. Dancers often have elaborate costumes and
decorated headdresses, such as this young Balinese dancer.

Marshall Cavendish Corporation
99 White Plains Road
Tarrytown, NY 10591
Website: www.marshallcavendish.com

© 1990, 2002 by Times Media Private Limited
All rights reserved. First edition 1990
Second edition 2002

Originated and designed by
Times Books International, an imprint of
Times Media Private Limited, a member of the
Times Publishing Group

Printed in Malaysia

Library of Congress Cataloging-in-Publication Data:
Mirpuri, Gouri.
   Indonesia / Gouri Mirpuri.
      p. cm. — (Cultures of the world)
   Includes bibliographical references and index.
   ISBN 0-7614-1355-3
   1. Indonesia—Juvenile literature. [1. Indonesia.] I. Title.
II. Series.

DS615 .M54 2001
959.8—dc21   2001028607
6 5 4 3

CONTENTS

Little Javanese girls in costume.

The traditional costume of the East Timorese.

INTRODUCTION

KNOWN FOR CENTURIES as the fabulous Spice Islands in the East Indies that provided Europe with exotic spices and priceless treasures, Indonesia today is a country with a variety of landscapes and lifestyles. It is a country with enormous diversity.

Oil-rich Indonesia was geared up to develop into a prosperous nation when the economic crisis hit it hard in 1997. This was immediately followed by political unrest, the decision of East Timor to withdraw from Indonesia, and a resurgence of factionalism. Today, the very survival of Indonesia as we know it is in question.

This book helps us better understand the Indonesian nation and its culturally diverse peoples. It is part of the book series—*Cultures of the World* that takes a look at people and their lifestyles around the world.

GEOGRAPHY

INDONESIA, the largest archipelago in the world, lies along the equator at the crossroads of Asia and Australia. This strategic position has greatly influenced its cultural, social, political, and economic life.

A NATION OF ISLANDS

Indonesia is a nation of 13,670 islands stretching over 3,200 miles (5,150 km) between the Indian and Pacific oceans, a distance greater than the width of the United States. Its total land area is almost three times the size of Texas, or two and one-half times the size of Australia. As 80 percent of the country's territory is in fact water, Indonesians refer to their country as *Tanah Air Kita* ("tah-nah ah-yayr kee-tah"), which literally means "Our (Nation of) Land and Water."

Above: **Mount Bromo, an active volcano in Java.**

Opposite: **Besides luxurious rain forests such as this, one can also find monsoon and montane forests with chestnuts, laurels, and oaks; alpine meadows; and mangrove swamps on the Indonesian archipelago.**

Indonesia's five main islands are Sumatra (which is slightly larger than California), Java (almost the size of New York State), Kalimantan (the southern extent of the world's third largest island—Borneo), Sulawesi (about the size of Great Britain), and Irian Jaya (the western portion of the world's second largest island—New Guinea).

Only 6,670 of Indonesia's islands are inhabited. These vary in size from rocky outcrops to larger islands, but many are so small that they do not even have a name.

Right: **An aerial view of terraced rice fields on the alluvial plains of Java. The soil, formed by volcanic ash and debris, is one of the most fertile soils in the world.**

Below: **The hundreds of volcanoes found in Indonesia not only dominate the landscape but also alter its size and soils by spewing forth millions of tons of ash and debris at irregular intervals.**

GEOLOGICAL HISTORY

The Indonesian islands were formed during the Miocene period, about 15 million years ago, seemingly a long, long time ago but only yesterday on the geological time scale. Most of Indonesia's volcanoes are part of the Sunda arc, which is a 1,864 mile (3,000 km) long line of volcanoes extending from northern Sumatra to the Banda Sea. Most of these volcanoes are the result of subduction of the Australia Plate beneath the Eurasia Plate.

Indonesia is located in one of the most volatile geological regions in the world. The mountainous spine, which runs right through the archipelago, contains hundreds of volcanoes, 220 of which are still active, with 76 recorded eruptions. Wherever you go in Indonesia, you are unlikely to lose sight of the regions' huge, conical-shaped mountains, which often have smoke billowing from them. Located on the Pacific Ocean's "Ring of Fire," Indonesia experiences about three tremors and earthquakes a day and at least one volcanic eruption a year.

The ash and debris regularly spewed out by the volcanoes are washed down and deposited in the alluvial plains. This whitish ash deposit is so rich in chemicals that it has produced some of the most fertile soils in the world. It has been said that one can push a stick in the ground and it will soon sprout leaves! Three rice crops can be produced in a year without the use of fertilizers, providing the staple food for one of the most populous countries in the world.

THE BIG BANG

On August 26th and 27th, 1883, the volcanic island of Krakatoa erupted in what was one of the most cataclysmic explosions in history. Imagine an explosion so tremendous that:

- It blew all 8.8 square miles (23 sq km) of the island of Krakatoa away.
- It produced a detonation which was heard in Australia, 2,200 miles (3,540 km) away.
- It threw out nearly 5 cubic miles (21 cubic km) of rock fragments and ash, which fell over 300,000 square miles (800,000 sq km).
- A tsunami, reaching a height of 120 feet (37 m), followed it and killed about 36,000 people on the adjacent shores of Java and Sumatra.
- A series of tidal waves was triggered, reaching as far away as South America and Hawaii.
- It produced an ash cloud that was reported to have reached 50 miles (80 km) high. Fine dust from this cloud caused spectacular sunsets all over the world for the next year.
- It was pitch black for two and a half days in the surrounding regions.

Although Krakatoa was totally blown apart in the 1883 eruption, continuing volcanic activity caused a growing cone of volcanic ash to emerge above sea level by 1928. *Anak Krakatoa*, or "Child of Krakatoa," had reached a height of 622 feet (190 m) above sea level by 1973. Seismologists are constantly monitoring this young volcano, while geologists and biologists study the life forms that have since evolved on this island.

THE WALLACE LINE

In the 1850s, a British naturalist named Alfred Russel Wallace exploring the region noticed that the Indonesian archipelago appeared to have zones of different flora and fauna. He was especially struck by the existence of clear boundaries within which one could find plants and animals typical of the Asian (or Oriental) mainland, those that were associated with Australia, and another zone that had another category of plants and animals. Although many zoogeographers today no longer consider Wallace's Line a regional boundary, it does represent an abrupt limit of distribution for many major animal groups and regions of fauna.

A map of Indonesia showing the vegetation zones.

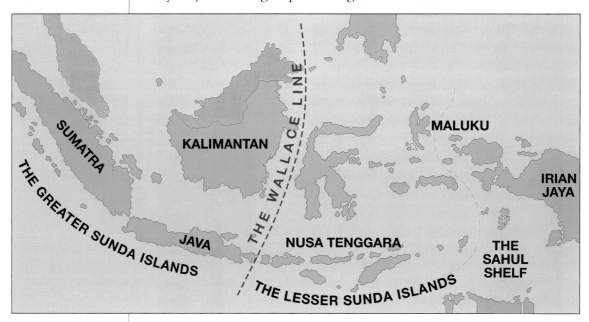

Left and below: **Flora and fauna east and west of the Wallace line are different. The one-horned Javan rhinoceros is similar to animals of the Asian mainland as the Sunda Shelf was once connected to it. The vegetation of the Moloccas (Maluku) islands** (below) **is typical of the Lesser Sunda region.**

One possible explanation for these boundaries is that during the last Ice Age, sea levels dropped so low that the islands on the Sunda Shelf— Borneo, Sumatra, Java, Bali, and some islands on the Lesser Sunda chain— were joined to the Asian mainland. Thus, the islands may have once formed a single land mass that was connected to the mainland. If one looks at a map of the island of New Guinea, it appears to fit neatly into northern Australia like a piece in a jigsaw puzzle. It sits on the Sahul Shelf, which is a northeastern extension of the Australian continental mass. This may be why animals that one associates with Australia, such as tree kangaroos and wallabies, can be found here.

In between the Sunda Shelf and the Sahul Shelf lies the Lesser Sunda region. A unique feature of this region is that it contains animal species not found anywhere else in Indonesia. This is because the Lesser Sunda region is separated from the other islands by deep sea trenches which are 24,442 feet (7,450 m) at their deepest. Hence, even when sea levels fell during the last Ice Age, this region remained isolated.

CLIMATE

Since Indonesia straddles the equator, it experiences the typical year-long hot and humid weather pattern of tropical countries. Afternoon thunderstorms are common.

Indonesia has only two seasons, and even these are not extremes. The "dry season" lasts from June to September; the "wet season" is from December to March. During the dry season, the islands come under the influence of winds from the southeast. The wet monsoon season brings rain from northeasterly winds, moisture-laden after traveling over the South China Sea.

"Rain" is sometimes too mild a word. During the monsoons, such tremendous walls of water explode from the sky that it is like standing under a huge waterfall! Rainfall can occur at any time of the year and it is even wetter in the mountainous areas, where it becomes hard to distinguish between the wet and dry seasons. It never seems to stop

raining, in Sumatra and Kalimantan!

Temperatures average about 81°F (27°C) and vary only according to altitude. Coastal plains experience temperatures of a tolerable 80°F (27°C), although exposure to the noonday sun can result in a bad sunburn. As you go higher, the temperature drops by 2°F (1.1°C) every 656 feet (200 m), resulting in a very pleasant 68° to 72°F (20°C to 22°C) in the highlands. Many Indonesians frequently escape to the mountains to spend their vacations "cooling off" from the heat of the lowlands. Some unusual contrasts exist. The famous Mandala Mountain in Irian Jaya is snow-capped in spite of being on the equator.

The snow-capped Mandala Mountain in Irian Jaya. Part of the Central Range, which is 311 miles (500 km) long, it is one of three ice areas. The other two are Mount Jaya and Ngga Pilimsit.

13

FLORA

Most of Indonesia is covered in evergreen equatorial rain forests. However, one is just as likely to find mangrove swamps with their looping aerial roots (in eastern Sumatra) and large tracts of arid savannah grassland (in the Lesser Sunda Islands). At higher altitudes, there are alpine meadows with chestnut, laurel, and oak trees that are more commonly found in countries with temperate rather than tropical climates.

The abundant rainfall and high humidity have produced some of the densest forests in the world. These forests are also self-fertilizing as the plants decompose and form rich humus very quickly after they die.

Indonesian flora is not only abundant but also exotic and incredibly diverse, with over 40,000 species recorded to date. About 6,000 species of plants are known to be used directly or indirectly by the people. Indonesia has some of the world's richest timber resources

ONE OF THE LARGEST FLOWERS IN THE WORLD

Found only in the jungles of south-central Sumatra, the immense *Rafflesia arnoldii* leads a parasitic existence on plant roots and stems. The plant has no leaves but its bud bursts open every couple of months to reveal five huge dark red petals with white specks. This is the world's largest bloom, which can measure about 1 yard (0.9 m) across and weigh up to 24 pounds (11 kg).

One species of plant found in the equatorial rain forests is the parasitic *Rafflesia arnoldii.*

and the largest concentration of tropical hardwood. It has more than 3,000 valuable tree species, including durian, teak, ironwood, rattan, ebony, sandalwood, camphor, clove, and nutmeg. Kalimantan and Java are centers for timber operations, where meranti and teak grow, respectively.

Among its flowers and plants are some 5,000 species of orchids ranging from the largest of all orchids, the tiger orchid, to the tiny *Taeniophyllum,* which is edible and used in medical preparation and handicrafts. Also found in Indonesia are exotic plants such as the carnivorous pitcher plant that traps insects in its liquid-filled cup and extracts their nutrients, and the strange parasitic creepers that include the strangler fig, with aerial roots that eventually strangle the tree on which it grows.

FAUNA

Indonesia boasts an incredible variety of wildlife. It is home to 12 percent of the world's mammal species, 16 percent of the world's amphibian and reptile species, 17 percent of the world's bird species, and 25 percent of the world's species of fish.

Its birds and animals include the one-horned rhinoceros of Java; the brilliantly colored bird of paradise that cannot fly; the tiny Lesser mouse deer which stands one foot (30 cm) tall; the ancient Komodo dragon; the Bali starling with silky snow-white feathers, black wing and tail tips; tigers, tapirs, marsupials such as bandicoots and cuscuses, peacocks, kuau, anoa, and numerous other animals.

Various conservation programs have been initiated to halt the threat to the orangutan (literally "man of the jungle") with a blazing orange shaggy coat.

Many animal species can only be found in one region and have become extremely rare. The remaining single-horned Sumatran rhinoceros are confined to the Kulon Peninsula National Park in Java. Another endangered species is the orangutan from Borneo and Sumatra. Orangutan rehabilitation centers have been set up at Mount Leuser National Park in northern Sumatra, and in a game preserve in southern Kalimantan. Other endangered animals in Indonesia include the siamang, Javan rhinoceros, banteng, Malay tapir, tiger, sunbear, leopard, and elephant.

Indonesia's insect kingdom is just as fascinating, including giant walkingsticks which can grow as long as 8 inches (20 cm), walking leaves, huge atlas beetles, and lovely luna moths.

Indonesia's complex coral reefs and marine ecosystems boast rich marine life, ranging from big game fish—such as marlins, tuna, barracuda, and wahoo—to whales, hammerhead sharks, and manta rays.

THE LARGEST LIZARD IN THE WORLD

Although dinosaurs are extinct, their latter-day relatives, the fierce Komodo dragons (*Varanus komodoensis*), have survived for millions of years in Indonesia, on the islands of Komodo and Rinca. These huge lizards can measure up to 10 feet (3 m) long and weigh 300 pounds (135 kg). They have long scaly bodies supported on short muscular legs, massive tails, and razor-sharp teeth. They eat smaller members of their own kind and occasionally attack and kill human beings, but mainly feed on carrion. Historians believe the mythological Chinese dragon may have been fashioned after this creature, whose long, forked, blazing orange tongue seemed to resemble fire.

Almost extinct because of collectors, in captivity they usually become fat and then die, but in the wild they can live up to 100 years.

HISTORY

PREHISTORIC REMAINS DISCOVERED in Indonesia show that one of the earliest humans lived in Java. Fossils of the famous prehistoric "Java Man," discovered in 1891, date back some 500,000 years.

HISTORIC MIGRATIONS

The first modern people in Indonesia were dark-skinned, wooly-haired, pygmy Negritos, who arrived about 30,000 to 40,000 years ago. They were followed centuries later by the Australoids who were also dark-skinned and wooly-haired but had broad, flat noses and pronounced brow ridges. Between 3,000 and 500 B.C., both these groups were driven into the highlands and jungles by the migration of Mongoloid peoples from the northern Indochina region: the Proto-Malays and the Deutro-Malays.

The Proto-Malays, represented today by ethnic groups such as the Bataks and Dayaks, brought with them a Neolithic, or New Stone Age, technology. They lived in village settlements, domesticated animals, and cultivated crops. Remnants of their culture can be seen today in the megaliths found in Sumatra. The Deutro-Malays belonged to the true Mongoloid race and took over the best agricultural lands. Their descendants constitute the majority of Indonesia's ethnically diverse population.

Above: **A reconstruction of Java Man from skeletal remains. His distinctive features were believed to be large brow ridges, a robust jaw, and a small chin.**

Opposite: **It is believed that Java Man's descendants are the Papuans of New Guinea.**

19

THE HINDU-BUDDHIST KINGDOMS

Of all the foreign influences at work in Indonesia, the greatest impact was made by Indian culture and religion. In the first to fifth centuries A.D., the Indonesian ruling class, impressed with India's philosophical, religious, and cultural superiority, started to "Indianize" their own kingdoms. They invited Brahmin scholars to their courts, sent students to study in India, learned about astronomy and navigational techniques, figure sculpturing and textile dyeing, adopted numerous Sanskrit words, introduced spices such as cardamom and turmeric into their food, domesticated horses and elephants, and adopted new architectural styles.

A candi, or a religious monument, one of many dotting Central and East Java.

The two biggest changes were in the new social status of the rulers and in religion. The Indonesian aristocracy found they could control their kingdoms better once they introduced the Indian concept of a divine ruler with limitless powers—a descendant of a mythical figure or a reincarnation of the Hindu god Vishnu himself.

India's twin religions—Hinduism and Buddhism—began a peaceful coexistence in Java and Sumatra. Over a period of 1,000 years, Indonesia's history is that of the rise and fall of many Hindu and Buddhist kingdoms. By about the eighth century, there were two kingdoms: the Buddhist Srivijaya kingdom in

Sumatra, which ruled the seas and major marine routes for the next 600 years, and the Hindu-Buddhist Mataram and Sailendra kingdoms of central Java, which controlled inland rice production for a shorter period of time. In fact, Sumatra was called Swarna Dwipa, or "Gold Island," while Java was called Yava Dwipa, or "Rice Island." The Srivijaya kingdom was based on foreign trade and controlled the strategic Strait of Malacca. From here, spices, incense, and other rare goods were traded between China and India.

The Javanese Mataram and Sailendra kingdoms were more spiritually oriented. The rich soils and wet-rice agriculture supported a huge population, much of which was later employed for the building of the magnificent Borobudur and Prambanan temples. This peaceful coexistence of Hindus and Buddhists did not last long; after a turbulent 300 years or so, there emerged a powerful new Hindu kingdom in Java called the Majapahit. Established in 1294 in an area known for its *pahit* ("PAH-hit"), meaning bitter, maja fruit, this empire marked the golden age of Indonesian history. The Majapahit Empire united the whole of Indonesia and parts of the Malay peninsula, and ruled for two centuries. It was then that a true Indonesian identity emerged, and a unique Javanese art and culture developed and flourished.

Around the 14th century, this great kingdom went into decline and was invaded by the new Islamic state of Demak. The entire Hindu-Javanese aristocracy fled to Bali, leaving behind a rich Indian-Indonesian heritage.

Viewed from the air, Borobudur's famous silhouette resembles a giant mandala, or Buddhist prayer symbol. It combines symbols of circles (representing heaven) and squares (representing Earth).

Conservation work on Borobudur continues in laboratories to help maintain this magnificent monument.

THE COMING OF ISLAM

When Marco Polo visited Indonesia in 1292, he noted that Islam was already established in parts of Aceh in north Sumatra. The religion was brought by Indian traders plying the India-China trade route.

From Aceh, Islam spread to the rest of Indonesia along the trade routes and the paths of economic expansion. To help spread the religion, rulers placed the royal *gamelan* ("GAH-may-lahn") orchestras in meeting halls that were turned into mosques. People from the surrounding areas came to listen to the music and were converted in the process. By the 15th and 16th centuries, many Indonesian rulers had made Islam the state religion, persuaded by the desire to strengthen ties with the neighboring port of Malacca, which had then become the center of Islam and trade. The growing international Islamic trade network brought yet more power and wealth. Islam was also a more egalitarian religion than Hinduism. In calling for the equality of all men before God, it had great appeal to the common people.

In the 16th century the Islamic kingdom of Demak attacked the weakening Hindu Mataram kingdom in central Java, taking control of its rich lands and driving the Hindu elite east to Bali. The fall of this once-great empire was recorded by Muslim court chroniclers as "the disappearance of the light of the universe."

THE EUROPEANS

Attracted by the spices of the Far East, the Portuguese found their way to the spice islands of the Moluccas (Maluku) in 1509 and established trading posts. Their profits encouraged other European traders to come to the region. While the English explored the Malayan peninsula and the Spanish in the Philippines, the Dutch arrived in Indonesia.

Jan Pieterszoon Coen, an accountant, founded the city of Batavia in 1619. His motto was *Dispereet niet!* ("Do not lose hope.")

In 1596, four Dutch ships arrived at Banten in Maluku after a difficult 14-month voyage during which more than half the crew members died. The few spices they took back to Europe caused so much excitement that, over the next 10 years, 65 more Dutch ships came to Indonesia in search of spices.

The Dutch soon established a strong foothold in Jayakarta (modern Jakarta), which they renamed Batavia. They started sinking the ships of any other country found in Indonesian waters, forcibly took over the spice islands of Banda, and, after more bitter, bloody fighting, gained control of the clove-producing Celebes Island, known as Sulawesi today.

By the end of the 17th century, the Dutch controlled not only the spice trade but also monopolized the production of coffee, sugar, indigo, pepper, tea, and cotton on several islands. The powerful Dutch East India Company

Right: **A 19th century Dutch painting of early Batavia by P. Lanters.**

Below: **A slave market in old Batavia. The slaves were worked hard and cruelly punished.**

(VOC in Dutch initials) was established to manage this trade and the huge profits from it. Headquartered in Batavia, it employed a large army and many servants.

In the 17th and 18th centuries, the Dutch expanded their control over all of Indonesia, which became known as the Dutch East Indies. On the island of Java, peasants were forced to grow export crops, making large profits for the VOC. This domination was achieved at great military expense, however, due to the constant resistance of the local people. This experience finally proved too costly. By 1799, the VOC went bankrupt in what was perhaps the largest commercial collapse in Indonesian history.

For a short time between 1811 and 1815, Indonesia came under British rule, but then reverted to Dutch rule.

THE NATIONALIST MOVEMENT

The Dutch did little to educate the Indonesians. Ninety percent of the local population was not educated at all. By the 1920s, a handful of colleges were opened, and some Indonesians were sent to Holland to be educated. When these scholars returned, they began agitating for freedom.

Raden Ajeng Kartini (1879–1904), Indonesia's first woman liberator and one of the country's most honored national heroes.

Two of Indonesia's important national heroes were Dipo Negoro and Raden Adjeng Kartini. In the early 19th century, Dipo Negoro, a very popular Javanese prince, fought a guerrilla battle against the Dutch for five years, which cost 200,000 Javanese and 8,000 European lives, mostly through starvation and cholera. Luring him with the bait of negotiations, the Dutch eventually arrested and exiled him in 1830, thus crushing the resistance.

Raden Adjeng Kartini was less fiery but equally admired. The daughter of a Javanese aristocrat, she was given the opportunity to attend a Dutch school. She was concerned by the impact of colonial rule and the denial of higher education to Indonesians, and by the limited roles available for Indonesian women. In the early 1900s, she wrote a series of powerful yet sensitive letters to her Dutch friends in Holland that, when published, caused a stir in the foreign community.

In 1927 the Indonesia National Party (the PNI) was formed under the leadership of a former engineer named Sukarno; it demanded independence from the Dutch. Sukarno was a gifted speaker and charismatic leader. He became so powerful that he was soon arrested and exiled. At this time the concept of an Indonesian nation was proclaimed in the famous Youth Pledge of 1928: "One People, One Language, One Nation."

JAPANESE OCCUPATION

Independence still seemed a long way off. When the Japanese arrived during World War II, the Indonesians, thinking this signified liberation from Dutch oppression, welcomed them with open arms. The Japanese began a ruthless exploitation of the East Indies. During the three and one-half years of Japanese occupation, numerous atrocities were committed, from the use of mass slave labor in the jungles of Burma and Malaya to starvation in Indonesia when the entire rice crop of Java was exported to Japan.

In order to increase their power and to spread propaganda, the Japanese promoted the Indonesian language, Bahasa Indonesia, as the national language. They also tried to unite the scattered islands by supporting the nationalists. Both these moves backfired. The confidence this gave the people prompted the nationalist leaders, Sukarno and Mohammed Hatta, to declare Indonesia's independence on August 17, 1945, just one week after the second atomic bomb destroyed Nagasaki in Japan.

At the end of World War II, the Dutch tried to regain control of Indonesia. However, by December 1949, under pressure from the United Nations and Indonesian nationalists, the Dutch finally recognized Indonesia's independence.

Monumen Lubang Buaya, the memorial for the army officers brutally executed and thrown into a crocodile hole *("lubang buaya")* in September 1965. Thousands were killed in the anarchy that followed. Today this period is still remembered as the darkest in Indonesia's history.

INDEPENDENT INDONESIA

The years following independence were not easy, with over 169 parties struggling for power. In 1959 Sukarno declared martial law and established his policy of "Guided Democracy." During this period of intense nationalism and anti-colonialism, the West was blamed for all of Indonesia's woes. In 1965, dubbed "The Year of Living Dangerously," a coup was staged by the Communists. On the night of September 30, members of the Communist Party and a group of young army radicals kidnapped, tortured, and brutally killed six leading generals and an officer. There are conflicting reports of what happened that day, but within a few hours General Soeharto had moved in to crush the coup.

Right: **Unlike his predecessor Sukarno, who had a very flamboyant personality, President Soeharto maintained a low profile, preferring to stay in his modest home in Jakarta instead of the presidential palace.**

Below: **Sukarno, Indonesia's first president.**

The next 12 months saw hundreds of thousands of Communists killed and thousands more imprisoned. Students demonstrated on the streets, demanding the banning of the Communist Party and lower prices for food and other essentials. Finally, on March 11, 1966, the once all-powerful Sukarno was persuaded to sign a document that would stop the riots and hand the presidency over to General Soeharto.

With political peace came economic prosperity. Upon his appointment, Soeharto quickly imposed martial law and banned the Communist Party. He also broke ties with Communist China and the U.S.S.R. and revised Indonesia's foreign policy.

Within Indonesia, the entire civil service was reorganized. The economy gradually set out on a path of high growth through sensible policies aimed at controlling foreign investments, boosting oil exports, slowing population growth, and increasing food production. The inflation rate was reduced and the rupiah stabilized. Soeharto's economic "New Order" had begun.

28

REFORMASI: A NEW ERA

The economic crisis which hit in 1997 left Indonesia on the edge of bankruptcy. Rising prices led to riots and looting, and anti-Chinese sentiments resurfaced. Soeharto was re-elected in February 1998 in the face of open opposition. Street demonstrations were met by tanks and bullets. In three days, over 6,000 buildings in Jakarta were damaged and some 1,200 people died. The Chinese bore the brunt of the violence. Soeharto's ministers called for his resignation and the Presidency was vacated on May 21, 1998, ending 32 years of Soeharto's rule.

A period of interim rule by Vice President Habibie did not stop the violence, which spread to the outer islands and took on a Muslim-Christian aspect, rare in usually tolerant Indonesia. On August 30, 1999, the East Timorese voted for independence in a referendum. In an attempt to find a new head of state who would appeal to the diverse elements emerging in Indonesia, Abdurrahman Wahid (Gus Dur) was elected fourth president of Indonesia on October 20, 1999. Abdurrahman, a respected Muslim moderate and chairman of the biggest Muslim organization, Nahdlatul Ulama, accepted nationalist Megawati Sukarnoputri (Sukarno's daughter) as Vice President. This compromise leadership did not please the conservative Muslims in separatist-minded Aceh, where violence continued.

While secessionist groups maintain their calls for independence, changes to Indonesia's political landscape have led to a breakdown in central control by the military. Embattled President Abdurrahman Wahid has been implicated in two financial scandals, and the students who helped to oust President Soeharto are up in arms in protest against corruption. The complex matrix of Indonesian politics threatens to unravel as Wahid faces an uncertain future. This new era is still far from developing a character acceptable to all Indonesians.

In January 2000, Abdurrahman Wahid's personal masseur allegedly obtained Rp 35 billion from the State Logistics Agency (Bulog), acting on an order from the president. In the same month, Wahid allegedly received US$2 million in personal donations from the Sultan of Brunei to be used for humanitarian work in Aceh. The two scandals, known respectively as "Buloggate" and "Bruneigate" came to public attention a few months later. Wahid has denied any wrongdoing.

GOVERNMENT

INDONESIA HAS A presidential system of government.

THE NATIONAL GOVERNMENT

The highest political body is the Majelis Permusyawaratan Rakyat (MPR, or People's Consultative Assembly), which elects the president, decides on policies, and issues decrees which have the effect of law. The MPR consists of 700 members, 500 of which are legislators directed elected by the populace every 5 years. These legislators also form the Dewan Perwakilan Rakyat (DPR or House of Representatives). The other 200 comprise appointed regional delegates and those from different interest groups, representing interests such as women, children, sports, business, and religion.

DPR members belong to the main political parties which, since the 1999 general election, comprise: Golkar (Joint Secretariat of Functional Groups), PPP (the United Development Party), PDI-P (the Indonesian Democratic Party-Struggle), PKB (the National Awakening Party), and PAN (the National Mandate Party).

The president, who is both head of state and chief executive, is elected to a five-year term. The president appoints a Cabinet to carry out state policy and is responsible to the MPR.

Opposite: **Vice President Megawati Sukarnoputri (left) of the Indonesian Democratic Party-Struggle and President Abdurrahman Wahid (right) of the National Awakening Party at a prayer rally in Jakarta on July 25, 1999.**

THE MPR (People's Consultative Assembly)

THE PRESIDENT

THE CABINET

THE MINISTERS

THE DPR
(House of Representatives)

THE REGIONAL LEVEL

Indonesia is divided into more than 30 provinces, including the three special territories of Jakarta, Yogyakarta, and Aceh. Each province has a capital and is headed by a governor. The provinces are further divided into districts, each with a *bupati* ("boo-PAH-tee") or regent as its head. Within the districts are hundreds of little towns and villages, headed respectively by the *walikota* ("WAH-lee-koh-tah") or mayor and village headmen. The village headman is guided by the village council of elders.

The hierarchy of power.

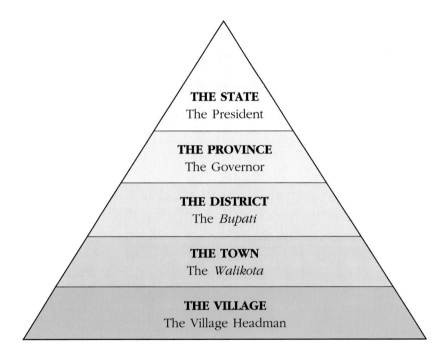

THE STATE
The President

THE PROVINCE
The Governor

THE DISTRICT
The *Bupati*

THE TOWN
The *Walikota*

THE VILLAGE
The Village Headman

DECISION-MAKING

Whether at the topmost level of state or down in the tiny villages, all Indonesians make decisions in a similar manner. This is through *musyawarah* ("moo-SHU-AH-rah"), or consultation, and *mufakat* ("moo-FAH-kaht"), or discussion, until a consensus is reached. It can be a long and tiring process. The government emphasizes a system of consensus so that everyone is happy with the final result.

In Indonesian-style democracy, everyone's views are heard and considered and taken into account to reach a solution that is acceptable to all concerned.

Another important system of administration in Indonesia is based on the concept of *gotong royong* ("goh-TOHNG roh-YOHNG"), where everyone works together to achieve a common goal. The *gotong royong* system means that the entire community has a joint responsibility to cooperate with each of its members. Whether it is a flood, volcanic eruption, or just harvest time, everyone in the village volunteers to help a needy neighbor. In this way, anyone in trouble gets help, and the job gets done much more quickly.

PANCASILA DEMOCRACY

Just as the United States has its Bill of Rights, Indonesia has its *Pancasila*, or the Five Principles. Indonesian democracy is based on these principles, and is called *Pancasila* democracy. These principles, declared by President Sukarno in 1945, are a combination of ideas with a focus on traditional village customs.

Pancasila now serves as a way of life for Indonesia's millions who learn about it in school, when they work for the government, and throughout their lives. In fact, the entire first week of the new school term is called "*Pancasila* Week."

Each of the five *sila,* or principles, of *Pancasila*, the state policy, is represented on the coat of arms.

The golden eagle or *garuda* represents creative energy and is a symbol from ancient Hindu epics. Gold symbolizes the greatness of the nation.

The shield stands for self-defense.

The equator, which passes through Indonesia.

The national motto, "Unity in Diversity," was first coined by a 15th-century saint.

The number of feathers on the neck (45), a wing (17), and the tail (8) of the *garuda* represents the date of Indonesia's Proclamation of Independence, August 17, 1945.

The colors of the national flag, red and white.

PANCASILA, THE FIVE PRINCIPLES

Today, the values of *Pancasila* constitute the state policy and the life philosophy of all Indonesians.

The star.

1 **Belief in one supreme God**
Indonesians believe in a God and most follow one of four great world religions—Islam, Buddhism, Hinduism, or Christianity.

The unbroken chain of humanity (the circles represent women, the squares men).

2 **Humanitarian ideals**
Indonesians do not tolerate oppression, either physical or spiritual.

The banyan tree.

3 **National unity**
In 1928 Indonesia's youth pledged to have one country, one nation, and one language, binding together the diverse peoples of the archipelago.

The head of a wild buffalo

4 **Indonesian-style democracy**
There is discussion (*musyawarah*) and mutual assistance (*gotong royong*) to reach consensus (*mufakat*). It is also referred to as *Pancasila*-style democracy.

Sprays of cotton and rice.

5 **Social justice**
An equal distribution of welfare and the protection of the weak.

ECONOMY

INDONESIA IS ONE OF THE WORLD'S major suppliers of rubber and also a major exporter of petroleum, natural gas, oil, tin, plywood, and textiles. It also produces commodities such as coffee, tea, tobacco, copra, spices (cloves and nutmeg), and oil-palm products. Its labor force was 88 million in 1998 but is still mainly employed in agriculture.

The agricultural products Indonesia produces also include: rice, cassava (tapioca), peanuts, cocoa, copra, poultry, beef, pork, and eggs. Tourism and chemical fertilizers and food production also contribute to the economy. With some of the world's largest tracts of exploitable forest, Indonesia's timber industry has grown rapidly.

Indonesia made impressive progress economically during the years leading up to 1997. Between 1981 and 1997, the economy grew by an average of 6 percent per year. It dropped to zero in 1999 but recovered to about 4 percent in 2000.

Above: **This paper mill in Sumatra contributes to Indonesia's billion-dollar timber and plywood export industry.**

Opposite: **Harvesting rice in Indonesia is a community event.**

Economic reforms and liberalization transformed the country, stimulated growth and raised expectations. Until 1997, foreign investment was rising and the country's foreign debt was falling. However, all these gains were wiped out by the financial crisis of 1997, when inflation soared to 80 percent, millions lost their jobs, and large-scale poverty again reared its ugly head.

37

An oil refinery in Balikpapan. Because such a major portion of Indonesia's revenue is derived from oil, a drop in oil prices hurts the economy. However, with careful management and diversification into other industries, Indonesia is now less vulnerable to fluctuations in the price of oil.

SOURCES OF REVENUE

MINERALS AND ENERGY Indonesia has vast mineral and energy resources. A big money earner is oil and gas, accounting for 27 percent of domestic revenues in 1999. Petroleum refining is carried out by the state oil firm, Pertamina. The government is seeking to replace crude oil exports with exports of refined petroleum products and petrochemicals. Indonesia is also seeking to increase the production and exports of its liquefied petroleum gas.

Indonesia is also rich in tin, coal, iron, copper, bauxite, nickel, lead, gold, silver, manganese, zinc, titanium, and uranium.

INDUSTRY Industrial development has made great strides in Indonesia as a result of diversification to reduce the country's dependence on oil. Investment restrictions have been relaxed, and greater incentives are now offered to foreign investors to set up manufacturing plants in Indonesia. Indonesia has a light manufacturing sector involved in a wide range of products, from producing handicrafts to assembling foreign cars. It also has cement, fertilizer, timber processing, steel, and oil-related industries. Although signs of economic recovery from the 1997 crash are slight, there has been some recent expansion in the sectors of textiles, chemicals, electronics, and furniture.

AGRICULTURE Indonesia remains a largely agricultural country with the majority of the population working on the land.

Indonesia is one of the world's largest producers of rice. This is due to the fertility of its soils. The introduction of high-yielding varieties of rice in 1968 also helped. On the inner islands, most of the rice is grown on terraced *sawah* ("sah-wah") or wet rice fields, the traditional method of farming for the last 2,000 years.

On the outer islands, where the soils are not as rich and there is less population pressure on the land, *ladang* ("lah-dahng") or "slash and burn" cultivation is more popular. This involves clearing several acres of forest land, using it for planting crops for a couple of years, and then moving on once the soil is completely depleted. Environmentalists are concerned that this practice does not allow the soil to regain its fertility and leads to fires that rage out of control. The overuse of pesticides by Indonesian farmers has also led to a developing resistance of pests to pesticides and the elimination of natural predators that control these pests. For example, in 1986–87, an estimated

124–148,000 acres (50–60,000 hectares) of cultivated rice were lost to an outbreak of pesticide-resistant brown planthoppers.

Indonesia is the world's second largest producer of rubber after Malaysia, a top producer of cloves and coffee. Other agricultural crops grown are corn, cassava, soybeans, palm oil, tea, spices, and tobacco.

Left: The rich alluvial soils of the lowlands produce three rice crops every year from "wet rice" fields.

Below: Environmentalists are concerned that "slash and burn" techniques of farming will deplete the soil of nutrients.

TOURISM Indonesia's travel industry is growing. Some 5 million tourists visited Indonesia in 1999 as compared to about 4 million in 1995.

Bali, Java, and North Sumatra currently draw the most tourists. The government is encouraging the growth of the tourism industry by restoring ancient monuments such as Borobudur; by constructing new hotels, theaters, and art galleries in cultural centers such as Yogyarkarta; and by promoting the remoter islands, for example by opening an airstrip at Tana Toraja. Local and foreign entrepreneurs have also cashed in by opening hotels, restaurants, bars, and souvenir shops along seafronts.

FISHING AND FORESTRY As one would expect of an island nation, the fishing industry is important to Indonesia. Government efforts to promote this industry have been successful, and shrimp export revenues have become an important foreign exchange earner for Indonesia.

Although depletion in recent years has been alarming, Indonesia has the second largest forest reserves in the world after the Amazon jungle in South America. These reserves are largely on the islands of Sumatra, Kalimantan, and Irian Jaya, and are another source of revenue.

Islanders on Lembata in East Nusa Tenggara still hunt whales by harpoon.

ENVIRONMENT

INDONESIA HAS A VARIETY OF habitats and ecosystems rarely equaled in the world. Almost 60 percent of all tropical forests in Asia, and about 90 percent of Asia's virgin forests are found in Indonesia. This vast country contains mangrove swamps, glaciers in Irian Jaya, coral atolls in the Flores Sea, and dense rain forests in Kalimantan, Sumatra, and Irian Jaya.

Sadly, economic growth, massive population increases, and ecological disasters have thrown the environment into disharmony. At the birth of the 21st century, Indonesia had the dubious distinction of having the greatest number of endangered species in the world.

Deforestation has led to soil erosion in the uplands of provinces such as Java, South Sumatra, Lampung, South Sulawesi, and East Nusa Tenggara. Urban areas suffer from flooding, and inadequate sewage and waste disposal systems has led to air and water pollution. Many of Indonesia's major fishing grounds have been depleted and its rivers polluted.

The government has taken measures to conserve wildlife and the environment by setting up protected areas and parks, developing ecotourism, and directing programs to clean up water pollution. Foreign conservation groups are also increasingly active in wildlife conservation.

Above: **Dense rain forest in West Sumatra.**

Opposite: **The Northwall Firn ice mass on Puncak Jaya glacier in Irian Jaya.**

AN ENVIRONMENT IN DANGER

The population of Indonesia has increasingly eaten into its finite capital resources.

In recent years millions of Indonesians migrated from overpopulated areas of intensive rice cultivation to areas traditionally used for forestry. These transmigrants in many cases attempted to recreate the irrigated rice fields they left behind. To create new rice lands, slower growing hardwood forests and their particular ecosystems were destroyed. For example, over 3,861 square miles (1 million hectares) of peat forest were drained of water originally held in giant natural reservoirs, and animals have been hunted for food and profit to the point where they now provide very little of either.

Tractors clearing lowland tropical rain forest in West Kalimantan.

Vague land ownership laws have allowed individuals and companies to clear land as a way to stake a claim, and laws that regulate the use of fire for land clearing have not been enforced. The short-term lease of forest land to timber companies provides the exploiters with no incentive to manage the forests in a sustainable manner. The result has been the denudation of forests and an irresponsible use of fire. This combustible combination has resulted in large-scale forest fires that occur with alarming and increasing frequency.

THE DOLLAR FOREST

For thousands of years, the forest provided Indonesians with building materials, food, clean water sources, and fertile soil for small-scale cultivation. During all this time, it did not carry a price tag. Now it does.

Logging operations in Kalimantan.

In 1999 the export of timber and plywood combined earned US$4.7 billion. This is more than the $4.1 billion earned through the export of oil and oil products, and rivals Indonesia's biggest export earners: textiles, garments, and handicrafts, which together brought in US$5.6 billion.

The 1997 financial crisis hit Indonesia harder than most of the other East Asian economies. This was followed by civil unrest caused by the referendum and secession of East Timor from the republic. Foreign buyers, fearing an interruption of supply, shifted orders to other countries in the region. In these desperate economic times, concern for forest depletion has tended to take second place to its short-term value.

THE IRREPLACEABLE RATTAN

Indonesia's lucrative rattan industry accounts for some 90 percent of the world's rattan trade. Exploitation of this plant has increased dramatically in Indonesia, however, as supplies in neighboring Malaysia and Thailand dry up.

There are over 300 species of rattan palm in Indonesia but it, and its mini-ecosystem of martial ants, bees, wasps and beetles, is yet another Indonesian plant in danger of eventual extinction.

The thorny rattans are climbing palms that need the tall trees for support. Their seeds, only one per fruit, take up to six months to germinate on the shaded forest floor and require moist forest soil and a complex interaction of insects, fungi, and bacteria to survive. Indonesia's forest peoples eat the "hearts" of the rattans (the bunch of folded young leaves at the center of the plant) and extract red dye from the fruits. In addition to furniture, rattan is widely used for basket-weaving, walking sticks, fish traps, and suitcases.

FOREST ON FIRE

With increasing frequency, Indonesia's forests in Sumatra and Kalimantan have become victims of fires raging out of control. In 1983 some 13,510 square miles (35,000 square km) of forest were destroyed in Kalimantan. This was followed by fires lasting for months in both Sumatra and Kalimantan in 1991, 1994, and most notably in 1997, which was reported as the greatest ecological disaster the world had ever seen. Nearby Singapore and Malaysia lived for months under the pollution of the "great haze" and complained that Indonesia had not done enough to prevent or control its fires.

The tragedy is that these fires were largely preventable. The moist conditions and dense hardwoods found in a tropical rain forest do not burn easily. Only when the forests are degraded and thinned of their natural cover do they readily catch the flames from fires set by farmers burning their fields in preparation for the annual agricultural cycle.

The financial damage from the 1997 fires was estimated, by 2000, as US$4.5 billion. This wiped out the export earnings from forest products for one year. It also made an incalculable contribution to global warming and human suffering in Indonesia and its neighboring countries.

Indonesian servicemen trying to extinguish fires raging across central Sumatra in October 1997.

Soaring demand from pulp and paper companies, plywood producers, and saw mills have left Indonesia without enough trees to go around. The result is massive illegal logging operations that are wiping out forests the size of the US state of New Jersey every year—and the pace is accelerating.

WHAT IS BEING DONE?

The Indonesian government set up a ministry dedicated to the environment in 1993—the Ministry for the Environment. This ministry led programs to control pollution, such as the Clean River Program (*Prokasih Program Kali Bersih*), and the replanting of trees. Protected wildlife parks and areas were also set up.

The World Wildlife Fund (WWF) established itself in Indonesia in 1962 and greatly expanded its activities in the last decade of the 20th century. Its aim is to preserve what remains and to reverse the damage to the environment. On behalf of the government, it prepared the Indonesian National Biodiversity Action Plan in 1991 and, in 1995, signed a cooperation agreement with the Ministry of Environment. The WWF has 20 major projects throughout Indonesia. It was instrumental in expanding the national park network and nature reserves. There are now national laws governing the clearing of land by fire, logging, harvesting, and hunting or collecting animals and plants. It is hard to enforce such laws, however, and Indonesia's political and economic problems have tended to take priority over conservation problems. The WWF now works closely with farming communities and industry in an attempt to introduce a "culture of conservation."

The role of environmental non-government organizations (NGOs) is expanding rapidly under Wahid government. Other than The World Wildlife Fund, these local and foreign NGOs include The Indonesian Forum for the Environment (Walhi), The Leadership for Sustainable Development Foundation (Lead-Indonesia), and The National Consortium for Forest and Nature Conservation in Indonesia (*Konphalindo*). Research and development centers have also come to play an important role in environmental management.

THE DISAPPEARING ORANGUTAN

Everybody's favorite endangered species is the orangutan. Recent scientific analysis of DNA confirms that the orangutan is one of man's closest relatives. The 1999 World Wildlife Fund Orangutan Action Plan calculates that an increase of only one percent in adult mortality will lead to extinction within five decades. Outside of the world's zoos, orangutans exist only on the Indonesian islands of Borneo and Sumatra. To exist in their natural state, orangutans require large expanses of primary forest. Over-farming of rattan has removed much of the orangutan's keystone resource, and the great forest fires of 1997 have added to their plight.

In addition to rattan and other palms, orangutans eat sweet pulpy fruits, insects, young leaves, sap, honey, and mushrooms. Fires and forest exploitation patterns have disturbed the ecosystems that provide this diet. Orangutans have coped with hunger by migration and dietary change: stripping bark from trees to eat the softer interior. Reduction of fruit in their diet has led to a reduction in fertility.

Orangutans suffer an additional threat caused, ironically, by their resemblance to humans and the human desire to possess the cute and cuddly. Females are often shot in order to obtain their babies, which are sold as pets. Orangutans raised in captivity, ironically, pick up a range of human diseases and carry these to other orangutans in the forest.

INDONESIANS

INDONESIA IS THE FOURTH most populated country in the world—after China, India, and the United States—and its population was estimated in 2000 as 225 million.

POPULATION PRESSURES

The population distribution from island to island is uneven. More than 135 million people, some 60 percent of the entire population lives on Java, an island that accounts for only 7 percent of the total land area of Indonesia. So with over 2,500 people crammed into every square mile (1,000 people per square km), Java is the world's most densely populated agricultural land. With a population growing at 1.5 percent per year,

Java's population could double in 30 years unless strong measures are taken—measures unlikely to be popular with a politically active people. In contrast, Kalimantan, which accounts for over 25 percent of Indonesia's land area, is home to only 5 percent of the population. Bali and Madura also have high population densities.

About 70 percent of Indonesians live in rural areas. In fact, Indonesia has been called a nation of villages, having more than 60,000. However, Indonesia also has some of the largest cities in Asia. In 1999, Jakarta's

Above: **Java is one of the most heavily populated areas in the world. Over 135 million people live on an island about the size of New York.**

Opposite: **Indonesia has a young population: about 30 percent were under 20 years of age and about 6 percent over 60 in the mid-1990s.**

Overcrowding in the major cities has resulted in the development of slums, much like this one along the Ciliwang River in Jakarta.

population was 9.3 million. As Jakarta continues to grow, it is merging with the surrounding towns. By the year 2000, a huge megacity of some 17 million people had evolved called Jabotabek (this name is taken from the first two letters of Jakarta, and the neighboring towns of Bogor, Tangerang, and Bekasi).

Indonesia has a young population, with about one-third of the people under 20 years of age. This is due to the high population growth rate, especially among the poorer sections of society, where people have many children as an insurance for themselves in their old age. The average life expectancy is 65 years. By 2020, however, the number of Indonesians aged 60 years and above is projected to reach 11.4 percent of the total population—a future problem for policy-makers.

Indonesia's population problems have been dealt with in two ways: by controlling growth through family planning and by spreading distribution through a transmigration program. Its success in increasing the use of contraceptives is good news given the fact that Indonesia's labor force is also growing, including women in the childbearing age.

TWO IS ENOUGH

Population pressure is a problem in overcrowded Java and Bali. In these rural areas, farmers struggle to make a living from tiny plots of land. In the urban centers, the situation is worse, as millions are crammed into tiny shacks in congested slums along narrow back alleys.

To combat its population crisis, Indonesia has launched a family planning campaign. "Two is Enough" is the motto of the active National Family Planning Coordinating Board. The success of the program can be measured by the fact that 21.3 million couples were practicing some form of family planning by 1993, compared to only 400,000 in 1972. One factor that has helped is that the preference for boys is not as pronounced as in countries such as China and India. Family planning has become such an open topic in Indonesia that in the villages "King and Queen of Contraception" contests are held! In the cities it is perfectly normal to ask people what contraceptive method they use.

Transmigration has also been introduced to ease population pressures. First introduced by the Dutch in 1904, this involves resettling families from overpopulated Java to the underpopulated "outer" islands, especially Kalimantan and Irian Jaya. The government claims to offer this program voluntarily. Those who are moved are usually the poorest families from urban and rural areas. Once they reach their new homes, they are given 2 hectares (5 acres) of land, a house, one year's supply of food, basic farming tools, and seeds to start life afresh.

The 5 *rupiah* coin, the smallest denomination of money, depicts the country's population policy: a couple with two children.

53

ETHNIC HISTORY

The most fascinating feature of Indonesia is the incredible diversity of its people. It is a country where more than 300 different ethnic groups speak 250 distinct languages and have their own individual culture and customs. This is a land where four of the world's major religions are practiced—where prayers are offered to Allah (Islam), Shiva (Hinduism), Buddha (Buddhism), and the Christian God. Even the physical appearance of the people varies from region to region. They differ vastly in skin and hair coloring, hair type, and facial features.

There are two theories about how such a diverse group of people populated the Indonesian archipelago. One theory suggests that large groups of people migrated in waves to Indonesia over several centuries from the Asian mainland. The other theory is that there was no coordinated mass movement; instead, the various races that came to Indonesia did so in small groups, mixed and mingled with the local people, and, over several centuries, replaced the original inhabitants.

It appears that at least four distinct groups have migrated to Indonesia over the centuries: the Negritos, the Australoids, the Proto-Malays, and the Deutro-Malays. This migration must have been relatively easy because during the last Ice Age, the sea level was low enough for the islands of

the Sunda Shelf to be linked to mainland Southeast Asia.

The Chinese are among Indonesia's most recent immigrants. Although they are a tiny minority, they are an important part of society and control a large portion of Indonesia's wealth.

ETHNIC GROUPS

In this country of scattered islands, high mountains, and dense jungle, it is the sea that unites and the land that divides. Thus, it is common to find similarities among peoples on adjoining islands but differences between the peoples of coastal and interior regions.

Some stereotypes have arisen. People say: "...all Javanese speak softly and indirectly; all Bataks like to laugh, play the guitar, and are aggressive; all Balinese carve and dance...." In reality, one is just as likely to meet a loud Javanese, a serious Batak, or a Balinese who is not artistic.

The main groups are the Javanese (45 percent), followed by the Sundanese (14 percent), Madurese (7.5 percent), and coastal Malays (7.5 percent). Javanese have had the most exposure to outside influences as Java is the most developed of the Indonesian islands. Among other groups, such as the Dayaks in Kalimantan and the Irianese who live in remote areas, some may never have seen a foreigner.

Many of the peoples of Irian Jaya live in isolation from the modern world. Here a group is fascinated by a Polaroid picture of themselves.

The Caucasian-looking Acehnese are staunch Muslims. They are fine craftsmen and boat builders. Aceh, in north Sumatra, was a major trading center for centuries and the first point where Islam arrived in Indonesia.

The Badui are a fascinating people who live in the isolated highlands of West Java where they first fled to escape Islam. Here they live by strict beliefs all their own and are forbidden to take any form of transportation or learn writing, which is believed to have "secret powers." The white-robed "inner" Badui who live in the heart of the homeland are even more strict and are believed to have mystic and clairvoyant powers.

The isolated Dayaks, who have a rich tradition of art, live in longhouses along rivers in the jungles of Kalimantan. They use blowpipes for hunting and are animists—they believe that spirits dwell in many things, especially the life-providing river. Headhunting has only recently been stopped. Tattooing and wearing several metal earrings to elongate the ear lobes are regarded as beautiful.

The Balinese are Hindu and their religion determines much of their lifestyle. The preparations for elaborate temple, cremation, and other ceremonies take up most of their energies. Balinese art is world famous, with each village specializing in a particular creative craft.

The sturdy Bataks live in north-central Sumatra. Many Bataks are Christians, the largest Batak Christian group living around the picturesque Lake Toba. They are a proud, conservative people. Many are musically inclined and become singers and band leaders.

The Javanese constitute more than half of Indonesia's population. Java has always been the center of Indonesian history because its rich volcanic soils have supported a large population. This explains its highly developed culture, art, and language. Today, rural Javanese live in overcrowded villages and grow rice on tiny plots.

The Minangkabau are a matrilineal society where the women are the inheritors of the family's wealth and where the man lives with the woman's family after marriage. Divorce and remarriage are common, as is migration outside their native region of West Sumatra. There has always been a large Minangkabau representation in politics and government.

The Minahasa are Christians and largely Eurasian; that is, of European and Asian background. As their homeland, northern Sulawesi, is close to the Philippines, there are cultural links between the two. The Minahasa are well-known for their lavish feasts and large gatherings.

Ever since the 14th century, the Bugis have been the dreaded sea pirates of the Indonesian waters in their colorful, wind-driven sailboats. They are expert boat makers and have been traders (and pirates) for centuries. They sail without compasses, claiming they can "smell" tidal waves or approaching coral reefs.

The Torajanese are rugged, mountain-dwelling people famous for the eerie effigies of their dead that guard limestone cliffs in central Sulawesi. They worship the buffalo, wear headdresses of buffalo horns, sacrifice the animal on major occasions, and give buffaloes to the bride's family in marriages.

The Sundanese occupy the western third of Java. They are famous for their *wayang golek* (wooden puppets) and the haunting sounds of their hollow flutes.

Over a century ago, Chinese men came to Indonesia to work on Dutch plantations and in mines. Their wives were only allowed to join them in the early 20th century. Today, many of this largest ethnic group have local names, though the degree of assimilation varies. *Totok* Chinese are first-generation Chinese in Indonesia.

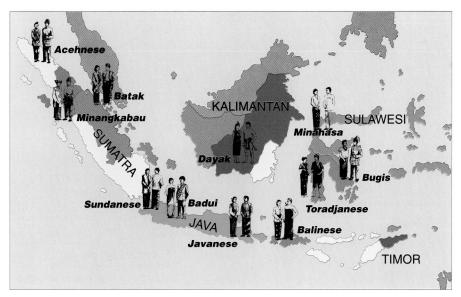

Acehnese
Batak
Minangkabau
SUMATRA
KALIMANTAN
SULAWESI
Minahasa
Dayak
Bugis
Sundanese
Badui
Toradjanese
JAVA
Balinese
Javanese
TIMOR

No. of persons (per square mile)

- less than 5
- less than 25
- less than 45
- less than 200
- less than 250

LIFESTYLE

INDONESIAN LIFESTYLE is determined by *adat* ("AAH-dut") or custom. This is an unwritten code of traditional behavior that is found in every city, town, village, and farm. It is not a part of religion, but it contains rules of conduct for almost every situation.

There are many *adat* or rules for different ethnic groups in Indonesia. Besides covering behavior and taboos, they also govern matters such as ownership of land, inheritance rights, marriage and death ceremonies, the type of food eaten, and the general way of life. All Indonesians practice some form of *adat*, though practices differ among groups. Western influence in music, fashion, movies, and junk food are diluting the importance of *adat*, especially in the cities where academic achievement and economic power are emphasized. However, *adat* still has an influence on an Indonesian's core customs and behaviors.

THE SOCIAL WEB

It is extremely important in Indonesia to conform to the group rather than be different. "Doing your own thing," or deviating from the accepted behavior, is considered embarrassing and unnatural.

The first allegiance is to the family. In Indonesia, however, the family extends to grandparents, uncles, aunts, first, and even second cousins. In the big cities, anyone from the same village is called *saudara* ("sah-hu-DAH-rah") or relative. The family provides emotional and financial support, and relatives can be relied upon to help out in many situations—from paying for a child's education or a grandparent's medical bill to emotional support in times of crisis.

After the family, Indonesians have obligations to a wider group of society; for example, the clan, village, mosque, neighborhood, and work-related organizations.

Opposite: **Family planning programs encourage women to have just two children. This policy is an attempt to curb the population growth of the fourth most populated country in the world.**

BEING A GOOD JAVANESE

Many aspects of Javanese culture have become associated with Indonesia since the Javanese are the country's largest ethnic group. Javanese culture has been influenced by Hindu culture, which has refined social behavior. Visitors are quickly struck by the intricate rules of etiquette and the concern with politeness.

The Javanese do not like anything startling or unpredictable to disturb their single, seamless vision of the world. Their existence is a calm and peaceful one. Nobody should upset this stability. When something unpleasant cannot be avoided, however, it is dealt with by maintaining an outward calm. Many foreigners are startled when the tragic news of a dying child or loss of property is told with a smile, or even a nervous laugh. No Javanese thinks it funny; a smile just masks the emotional upset.

Indonesians hate confrontation, preferring to hide negative feelings such as jealousy and anger. They do not complain or shout, but cope with stress by smiling and quietly withdrawing. If pushed beyond limits, however, an Indonesian can lose control or even run *amok* in blind anger, a word that originated in this region.

Even in conversation, a Javanese always strives to "maintain the peace." This often means speaking in a roundabout, indirect manner—to ask for a glass of water, a person might clear his throat and comment on how dry and dusty the day is; no one would upset a host by refusing an invitation, even if unable to make it to the party. It often takes foreigners several months before they understand "Java talk!"

The Javanese way of life is also seen in their elaborate rules of etiquette. It is very important to show correct form and politeness, especially to elders. People talk in low, calm tones with no dramatic arm gestures, even in times of great excitement. To Javanese, extreme emotions like uncontrollable laughter or wails of sorrow indicate lack of self-control and refinement.

"One has arrived, in Javanese, when one has come to enjoy making the obvious comment at the proper time in the appropriate tone."

—Ward Keeler, in Javanese: A Cultural Approach

UNIQUE CHARACTERISTICS

FLEXIBLE TIME Time is structured very differently in Indonesia. The day begins at sunset, so "last night" is considered earlier the same day. Indonesians have a laid-back approach to punctuality—a person can arrive between an hour to three hours late without causing offense. When you ask someone the time, it is rounded off to the nearest quarter or even half hour; there is no need to be exact.

BATHING Indonesians bathe at least twice a day, and the more water splashed around, the cleaner and better. In a typical bathroom one does not climb into the stone water storage basin or *mandi* ("MAHN-dee"). Icy cold water is splashed from this *mandi* over oneself for an invigorating bath, which leaves everything soaking wet.

Most rural homes do not have toilets and one simply uses a nearby stream. A squat toilet is usually a hole in the ground with footrests on either side. There is usually no flush system or toilet paper, as water is preferred for reasons of hygiene.

SICKNESS Most Indonesians prefer to have mild illnesses treated at home. They believe that sickness can be caused by *masuk angin* ("mah-SOOK AHNG-in"), literally "the entrance of wind." To protect against this, Indonesians wrap themselves in warm clothes. It is common to see workers wearing zipped-up black leather jackets under the intense midday sun.

To cure any illness due to *masuk angin,* oil is rubbed onto a person's neck and back with a heavy metal coin that is vigorously scraped along the skin. The deep red stripes that remain for a day or two actually look much worse than they feel.

INTIMACY Public displays of intimacy between people of the opposite sex are considered improper, though it is perfectly acceptable for friends of the same sex to walk hand in hand. Kissing in public is taboo.

Being treated for *masuk angin* by rubbing a coin along the body.

FORGIVENESS Asking forgiveness for any errors made is a part of the national ethic and the main feature of Javanese politeness. At Lebaran, the end of the fasting month, Muslims formally beg forgiveness for wrongdoings of the past year from family and friends. When leaving a job, the same is done of one's colleagues and superiors. The apology is always accepted gracefully and everyone starts off with a clean slate.

A *gamelan* performance during a *selamatan* at a royal court, reenacted for the benefit of tourists.

THE SELAMATAN

All Indonesians have in common the *selamatan* ("ser-lah-maht-ahn"). This communal thanksgiving feast celebrates turning points in an individual's life such as birth, circumcision, marriage, death, and the start or completion of a major project. It is also an indicator of a person's wealth and status, usually measured by attendance. Every effort is made to ensure this number is large. However, the feast can vary depending on the ethnic group, status, age (the young prefer to simplify things), and the wealth of the family.

The host provides the entertainment: a *gamelan* or *wayang* performance. Nowadays, taped music played on loudspeakers is also popular and creates a festive mood. Special ceremonial foods are prepared, incense burned, and Islamic prayers intoned. In the royal courts, even larger *selamatans* are held on religious occasions.

SEMANGAT, THE LIFE FORCE

Many things in nature are believed to contain a vital energy or life force called *semangat* ("ser-mahng-aht").

In a person, *semangat* is contained in the head, blood, heart, hair, and nails. Children are not patted on the head, which is considered sacred, and clippings of nails and hair are carefully disposed of, as these can be used for sorcery. A child's first haircut is a significant event, and tying together a few strands of the bride and groom's hair symbolizes the strength of their union. Headhunters believed that returning home with enemy heads augmented one's powers, just as the power of a *keris* (dagger) increased with the number of times it had drawn blood.

There are ritual precautions to appease the spirits contained in important crops such as rice. Clothes, sacred heirlooms, and jewelry are believed to contain the soul of the previous owner. The *semangat* of mountains, lakes, and old trees must also be handled with respect.

A chicken is sacrificed in a housewarming ritual to appease the spirits.

Due to the high infant mortality rate, children are guarded carefully from both natural and supernatural forces.

PREGNANCY AND BIRTH

The seventh month of a pregnancy is celebrated on most islands with a ritual bath for the mother-to-be. On Java there is a ceremony where the pregnant woman prepares a special spicy fruit salad and "sells" it to guests who pay for it with roof tiles. It is believed the sale teaches frugality to the child, and the taste of the salad indicates the baby's sex— sour for a boy and sweet for a girl.

Throughout her pregnancy the mother is given specially prepared food and not allowed to touch sharp objects such as knives and scissors, which might harm the child. No gifts are given for an unborn child as overzealous actions and words are believed to invite evil.

Once the child is born, it is guarded through its first five years. Every ethnic group has a different welcoming ceremony for the baby. In Java the destiny of the child is predicted by placing various objects like a book, pen, and some gold in front of the child to see which object attracts its attention first. Special threads with amulets put around the child's arms or neck protect it against evil, and daily doses of special infant *jamu* ("JAR-moo") or herbal medicine keep the child safe.

THE GROWING-UP YEARS

Children are particularly treasured in Indonesia because the country has a high infant mortality rate.

Babies are always kept slung comfortably and securely at the mother's hip in a long, narrow piece of *batik*, the *selendang* ("SER-land-dung"). A child can demand to be carried this way for several years, or at least until the arrival of the next child. In this *selendang* the child is fed on demand rather than by the clock.

Everyone in Indonesia has a certain status and knows his or her proper place. There is security in this knowledge and nobody wants to disturb the peace by upsetting this system. Children soon learn that, within the family, status is arranged in a hierarchical order according to age rather than sex, with the father being right at the top. Generally, mothers have a greater role in bringing up children, while fathers are more distant figures.

In the workplace, this carries over to the "whatever pleases the boss" philosophy of most Indonesians. *Bapak* ("BAA-pak") is the word for father, but it is also used for anyone senior in age or status. No effort is spared to please anyone occupying the father-figure position. The boss is told what he wants to hear, true feelings and facts are covered up, and arguing with superiors is considered rude. Direct eye contact may be misinterpreted as a challenge, so the Javanese speak to superiors with downcast eyes in as humble a stance as possible.

A child being carried in a *selendang*.

CIRCUMCISION

When Muslim boys reach the age of 11, they undergo circumcision to mark their passage into manhood.

In the past, they would anaesthetize themselves with icy cold water before the event. Today there are mass circumcisions using modern medical equipment in most villages.

Sometimes the boys are dressed up as princes and paraded through town on ponies or decorated *becaks* ("BAY-chucks") (three-wheeled pedicabs). A *selamatan* usually follows the circumcision ceremony.

A mass circumcision ceremony.

The child's attachment to an older relative—grandfather, cousin, aunt, or uncle—grows stronger than the bond with his parents. Often the grandparents take full responsibility, financial and otherwise, for one grandchild. Children in turn help out with household chores, though a grandson is pampered more than a granddaughter and is only expected to run the occasional errand.

Children are only considered grown-up once they get married. Until then, they live with their parents, help out financially with the household expenses, and fulfill the social obligations expected of them. Once they are married, the bride either lives in her husband's home, or the couple gets a place of their own. The exception is found in the Minangkabau matrilineal system in West Sumatra where the reverse occurs—the groom joins the bride's family. Titles, wealth, and family names are all passed down the female line. Men look after family heirlooms but it is the women who hold the keys.

Most Indonesian families are very close-knit and keep in contact, even when separated by a great distance. The annual family reunion takes place at Lebaran when, just like at Christmas, everyone comes together from all parts of the archipelago to celebrate and exchange news.

The bride feeding the groom—a ritual during a Javanese wedding.

MARRIAGE

In Indonesia everyone is expected to marry. In the rural areas, most Indonesians marry at a young age; in the cities, marriage takes place later. By the time a rural girl reaches the age of 19, she is probably not only married but also a mother.

Indonesians believe that eventually everyone will get married. Even a 60-year-old bachelor replies to the question, "Are you married?" with a standard *"Belum,"* ("BER-loom") meaning not yet. Muslim law permits a man to have up to four wives, but this is discouraged.

Wedding ceremonies are among the most elaborate and colorful occasions in Indonesia. The most ornate ethnic costumes are worn, and lavish gifts, including gold, money, fruit, and flowers, are exchanged. The bride and groom sit in regal style on ornate thrones placed on a raised platform and do not mix with guests except to say thank you when the guests file past to congratulate them. The number of guests invited to a wedding can range from a few hundred to over a thousand. Some families spend so much on wedding feasts that they end up in debt.

In Balinese weddings, the tradition is for the bride to be "kidnapped" by the bridegroom. The honeymoon precedes the actual wedding, which occurs about a month after the "abduction."

DEATH AND FUNERALS

Funeral ceremonies vary with the religion and customs of different people. A Muslim is buried within 24 hours of death and colleagues, friends, and relatives arrive within hours to pay their respects to the deceased, regardless of how close they were. There is no weeping as this is considered an indication of a weak soul and an invitation to spirits.

It is believed that when a person dies his spirit must be properly "managed" or it will cause havoc in the world of the living. To prevent the soul from returning to earth, some rites are designed to confuse it. In Sumatra, the body is sent out of the house through a small gap in the floor, which is then sealed. In Bali and Sulawesi, the hearse is jolted and jarred to prevent the spirit from finding its way back. For the soul to successfully make it to the land of the ancestors— usually in the form of a bird or insect—proper funeral rites are essential. Although these vary by region and ethnic group, they are almost always colorful and extravagant spectacles.

If a family cannot afford this expense at the time of death, the body is either kept wrapped in shrouds in the house or temporarily buried until enough money is saved for the rites. In the recent death of a Torajan royal person, the widow kept the embalmed body of her husband in the house for two years before having one of the most spectacular funerals ever. In Bali the bereaved wait for more deaths so they can have a joint cremation. The bones are then exhumed, cleaned, and given a proper send off.

A Balinese royal cremation. Funerals are very often expensive affairs, especially in Bali where the dead are cremated in elaborate ceremonies.

Torajanese houses, a replica of which is seen near the effigies of their dead, are shaped like boats and all face north. Their ancestors are believed to have come from that direction in similar vessels that they later pulled ashore and used as roofs.

The dead are never forgotten in Indonesia: among the Torajanese, eerie effigies of the dead line the cliff faces, their final burial place; in Irian Jaya, the skull and bones of the deceased are preserved; and all over Indonesia, graves or symbolic statues are carefully tended as they contain the benevolent spirits of ancestors.

RELIGION

FOUR OF THE MAJOR religions of the world are found in Indonesia—Hinduism, Buddhism, Islam, and Christianity. In 1998, 88 percent were Muslims, 5 percent Protestants, 3 percent Roman Catholics, 2 percent Hindus, and 1 percent Buddhists. These were introduced from overseas—Hinduism and Buddhism from India, Islam from Muslim traders from India and the Middle East, and Christianity from the Europeans.

These religions were absorbed into Indonesia, and yet did not erase the original animistic beliefs and traditional customs *(adat)* that had existed for centuries. These religions were layered one on top of the other, each layer interacting with but never quite replacing the one before it. As an Indonesian proverb puts it, "Religion comes in from the sea, but customs come down from the mountains."

Above: **Devotees at the Goa Lawah bat cave temple in Klungkung, Bali.**

Opposite: **Worshipers in prayer on Bali.**

The earliest system of belief was animism, or belief in spirits (ancestor worship) and in the hidden powers of natural objects like mountains, trees, rice, rain, and the sun.

Hinduism and Buddhism came later and intermingled with animism. Then, when Islam and Christianity arrived centuries later, these too were modified and adapted to fit with the existing mixture of *adat*, animism, and Hindu-Buddhist beliefs.

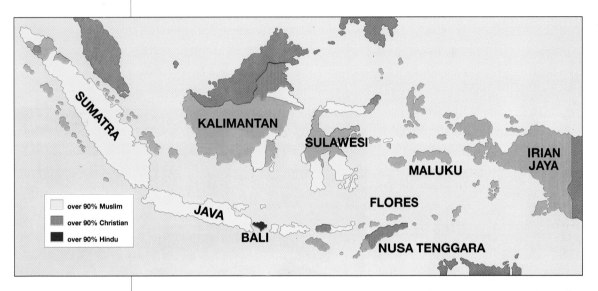

over 90% Muslim

over 90% Christian

over 90% Hindu

A map of Indonesia showing the concentration of religions among its people.

In the spirit of *Pancasila* (or Five Principles as mentioned in the Government chapter), there is freedom of religion. Religion is taken seriously and is an academic subject in school up to the second year of college.

Indonesia is the world's largest Islamic nation (with about 166 million Muslims). The Javanese and the Minangkabau of Sumatra make up the largest group of Muslims. Hinduism is mainly found on the island of Bali, while Christianity is found in pockets throughout the archipelago, such as in Sumatra, Kalimantan, Nusa Tenggara, and northern Sulawesi. Most Chinese are Buddhists and Confucianists.

In the Moluccas (or Maluku) Islands, which were at the center of the Dutch spice trade, small Christian communities originally converted by the Dutch can still be found. Flores Island has a Catholic population that was converted by Portuguese missionaries. In other areas, animist beliefs and practices predominate, especially in Kalimantan and Irian Jaya.

ISLAM

The national mosque of Indonesia is the Istiqlal Mosque in Jakarta.

Islam was first brought to Indonesia by Indian merchants, and later by Arab traders around the eighth century A.D. It was first established in Aceh in northern Sumatra, from which it later spread throughout Indonesia. Today, Java and Sumatra are the major Muslim areas. In other areas, the Muslim population is more scattered.

Islam preached the equality and brotherhood of man, an idea that appealed to people who were tired of being at the bottom of the rigid and hierarchical Hindu caste system. The few communities that resisted conversion, like the Badui and the Torajanese, fled to the interior as Islam spread through the islands.

Islam is a way of life, a practical rather than merely theoretical religion. Today it pervades every aspect of Indonesian life: loudspeakered mosques call the faithful to prayer five times a day; Friday, the Islamic holy day, is a half-working day; pigs are not very often found as they are seen as unclean; most public places have a little room set aside for prayer; public toilets are equipped with running for washing; men are allowed to take up to four wives at a time; and many Indonesians save money to make the *haj* ("HAAJ") or holy journey to Mecca.

Indonesia has a dual education system with both a general school system and a religious educational system. Islam is studied for a certain number of hours each week at all levels in the general school system.

The Islam practiced by individual communities ranges from the ultra-orthodox to nominal Muslims. The central Javanese practice an Islam mingled with animism and Hindu-Javanese mysticism. For instance, when a person is ill, the *dukun* ("DOO-koon") or folk doctor writes Islamic prayers on pieces of paper and dunks them in a glass of water for the patient to drink. Once drunk, the prayers supposedly fight the demon that is causing the illness.

Extreme religious conservatism is rare in Indonesia. Although the Acehnese are known to be strict Muslims, the rest of Indonesian Muslims have a more liberal attitude toward religion. Women, for instance, are much freer than their sisters in other Islamic countries. They do not wear facial veils but a very flattering low-cut blouse with a colorful, figure-hugging *sarung* ("SAH-roong") skirt instead. A husband has to get permission from his first wife before taking a second wife, and women are allowed to initiate divorce.

In societies like the Minangkabau of Sumatra, the matriarchal system exists in harmony with Islam's male supremacy. Under this system, the woman holds a family's wealth. Property is passed on from mother to daughter. Men do not inherit property. In the big cities, many women run successful businesses and are active in government.

THE CALL TO PRAYER

Muslims traditionally pray five times a day: at sunset, night, dawn, noon, and afternoon. The prayer times are published in the papers, broadcast over radio and television, and sounded in mosques all over the country.

Every Friday, Muslim men go to the nearest mosque for prayers, while women pray at home. A strict ritual must be followed before prayers begin.

First, the faithful must purify their bodies by washing. The hands are washed, then the mouth is cleansed by gargling and spitting. The face is then washed, followed by the lower arms up to the elbows. Then the head is moistened and the hair is combed with water. Finally, both feet are washed up to the ankles. All this is repeated three times in strict order and always starting with the right side. Menstruating women may not enter the areas of the mosque where prayers are said.

If a man touches a dog or a woman, goes to the bathroom, or "passes wind," he must repeat the entire ritual cleansing. The mind should also be purified.

Special clothes for prayers are also required. Women wrap themselves in a white gown from head to toe, while the men wrap a *sarung* around their waist.

In the mosque, there are also rules to follow. Shoes should be left outside. Muslims are also careful not to touch any unclean objects before and during prayer. Muslims greet fellow worshipers with the words *As salaam 'alaikum* ("ehs seh-LAHM eh-lei-koom"), meaning peace be with you, and respond with *Wa alaikum salaam* ("weh eh-LEI-koom seh-LAHM"), meaning and upon you, peace. Then the prayers begin with the muezzin's ("moo-EZ-in") call to prayer, which begins with *Allaho-akbar* ("ehl-LAH ho-EHK-behr"), meaning God is great.

HINDUISM

Hinduism arrived in Indonesia from India more than 1,500 years ago. Of all the religions that were transplanted in Indonesia, it made the greatest impact. Even the coming of Islam did not wipe out all remaining Hindu culture.

Many traces of its great past and influence still linger today, especially in Java and Bali. The palaces of Solo (Surabaya) and Yogyakarta are still cultural reminders of this long gone period; the characters and stories of Javanese classical dance and puppetry are based on the ancient Hindu epics, the *Mahabharata* and *Ramayana;* numerous Hindu ruins and ancient monuments, like Prambanan, are scattered all over the island; the Garuda, the mount of Lord Vishnu the Preserver, is Indonesia's national emblem; and Sanskrit, the language of Hinduism, is found in Javanese and Indonesian words, place names, and even the state motto, *Pancasila.*

Today, Indonesia's Hindu population is found on the island of Bali. Many of its people are the descendants of the Majapahits who fled from Java to escape Muslim invaders. The rich Hindu-Javanese culture, religion, and philosophy they brought with them were combined with existing Balinese animism, giving rise to today's unique Balinese Hinduism.

BALI'S HINDUISM

Balinese Hinduism is a unique combination of animist and Hindu beliefs. Hindu beliefs are seen in the Balinese belief in the Trinity of Gods—Brahma the Creator, Vishnu the Preserver, and Shiva the Destroyer—and the all-important cremation of the dead to release the spirit, enabling it to participate in the cycle of reincarnation. The Balinese knowledge of the Hindu epics forms the basis of many of their dance and other art forms.

The Balinese also practice ancestor worship, blood sacrifices, and mysticism. They often go into trances and are possessed by the gods and demons surrounding them in nature. They have numerous rites and sacrifices—hardly a day goes by without a ceremony aimed at keeping peace with the forces of nature. In fact, these endless colorful and elaborate temple ceremonies are a major tourist attraction.

A Balinese temple court-yard.

BUDDHISM

Devotees praying at the ancient monument of Borobudur, the largest Buddhist monument in the world. Most Buddhists live in Java and meet here for their most important annual festival —Waisak.

Hinduism and Buddhism have coexisted on Java for over a thousand years. Both originated in India, Hinduism being based on the religion of the original Aryan settlers, as expounded in texts such as the Vedas, Bhagavad-Gita, and Upanishads. Buddhists believe that life is full of suffering caused by desire, and that the way to halt this endless cycle of birth and death is through Enlightenment.

The Chinese and Tenggerese account for the major Buddhist sects. Other smaller Buddhist groups are also found in Java around the towns of Solo (Surabaya), Yogyakarta, and Cirebon.

Left: **A Catholic church.**

Below: **Traditional de-signs of carvings and tap-estry inside an Indonesian church.**

CHRISTIANITY

Despite being under European colonial rule for centuries, only 8 percent of Indonesia's population is Christian. The Christian population is scattered and found in pockets in certain parts of western Sumatra, the islands of Flores and Timor, northern Sulawesi, Moluccas, and in parts of Kalimantan.

The Christianity practiced by most ethnic groups, whether Protestant or Catholic, has intermingled with local beliefs, producing some interesting customs like the barefoot Easter procession in the dead of night in Flores, *gamelan*-led masses in Yogyakarta, and bull-sacrifices among the Torajanese Christians.

ANIMISM

Animism is a belief in the world of spirits, and belief that objects can have inner powers. These beliefs are found all over Indonesia where people's religious faith is influenced by spirits in such objects as rice, trees, rivers, rocks, the sun, and rain. Many people also believe that the spirits of dead ancestors live on.

Animist beliefs are mainly practiced by Indonesia's hill communities and other isolated social groups, especially in Kalimantan and Irian Jaya. However, even the Muslims, Hindus, Buddhists, and Christians of Indonesia retain some animist beliefs.

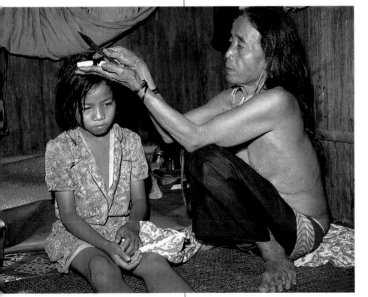

A lady shaman or witch doctor in Kalimantan curing a sick girl with an egg. It is believed the egg will "absorb" all "bad" spirits causing the illness within the girl.

Even the country's leaders believe in spirits and mysticism as they seek a divine spirit called the *wahyu* ("WAH-yoo"), which enters a person to provide guidance for making decisions.

GHOSTS AND GENIES In Java, when children do not sleep, they are told of the dreadful *way-way* ("way-way"), the "frightener" of small children. In Sulawesi, it is the *pok-pok* ("poke-poke"), the flying head, while in Bali, they fear the *leyaks* ("leh-YAHKS") who kidnap troublesome children.

Stories of ghosts, goddesses, demons, spirits, and genies abound. Buffalo heads are placed in the foundations of new buildings to appease the spirits, with priests often flying sacrificial heads to offshore oil rigs by helicopter for the same purpose. Witch doctors

exorcise evil from temples, swimming pools, cars, and hotels. Any transition in life—birth, circumcision, marriage, death—is accompanied by rituals and elaborate meals in the traditional *selamatan* ceremony.

Trees, flowers, hair, fingernails, blood, and weapons like the *keris* ("KEHR-is"), or dagger, are believed to possess a "life force" that must be carefully handled. Some communities worship spirits in stones, others sacrifice animals to volcanoes or perform trance dances.

And every Indonesian fears the queen of the South Seas, the spiritual wife of the sultan of Yogyakarta, who seizes anyone wearing a green swimsuit to become a soldier in her army. Most hotels along the south coast of Java conform to superstition by keeping one room locked and specially reserved for when the queen visits!

A spirit figure. Many Indonesians own talismans and spirit figures to protect them from evil.

AHLIKUNCI

"MAN"
AHLIKUNCI
MENERIMA
PESANAN
SEGALA
MACAM KUNCI
MOTOR
MOBIL

LANGUAGE

IN A LAND OF SUCH great ethnic diversity, Indonesia has 250 distinct languages and dialects spoken across the archipelago. Looking at individual islands, one may think that people in Java speak Javanese, people in Bali speak Balinese, and the Madura people speak Madurese. Within each island, however, different regions and ethnic groups have different local languages. On Java, for example, Javanese, Sundanese, and Madurese are all spoken and there are 15 major languages on Sumatra. Other languages spoken in Indonesia include Acehnese, Batak, Sasak, Tetum, Dayak, Minahasa, Toraja, Buginese, Halmahera, Ambonese, Ceramese, and several Irianese languages. Many of these languages are also spoken in different dialects, which makes for a more colorful culture and society. For instance, Sulawesi alone has 62 documented languages and countless more dialects.

Opposite: **A traveling keymaker. The sign advertises him as a master keymaker who can duplicate any key, including car keys.**

ONE PEOPLE, ONE LANGUAGE, ONE NATION

With such linguistic variety, it is easy to see why the Indonesian motto, *Bhinneka Tunggal Ika* ("BHEE-nay-kah TOONG-gahl EE-kah"), meaning unity in diversity, is of such significance to the issue of language. Since this number of languages could cause problems of communication, in 1928, Bahasa Indonesia (literally meaning "the language of Indonesia") was chosen as a unifying language to bridge the cultural and linguistic gap across all of Indonesia's scattered islands.

Javanese is the second most widely spoken language in Indonesia after Bahasa Indonesia. This is because almost the majority of the Indonesian population lives on Java, and because Java is still the focus of most of Indonesia's industry and commerce. Dutch is still spoken by some of the older generation but English is the first foreign language taught in schools. Even so, few people speak English well.

BAHASA INDONESIA

Bahasa Indonesia, the national language, is derived from Malay, which has been the language of trade throughout Southeast Asia for centuries. It is written in the Roman script and is one of the simplest languages in the world. It has no tenses, grammatical gender, tones, or articles, and its few plurals are made by simply repeating the word. It is easy to learn the language for simple communication, although the refined variety with its complex affix structure and strict grammatical rules is more difficult. It is a democratic language without the status markers present in Javanese, Sundanese, and Balinese. Also because it is a neutral language, it does not discriminate against the other languages found in Indonesia.

It was introduced as the national language of Indonesia in 1928 when Indonesian nationalist leaders realized that freedom from Dutch colonial rule also meant that they had to find a truly national Indonesian language. Previously, these nationalist leaders had been communicating in Dutch. In the famous "Youth Pledge" of 1928, three ideals were adopted: One Fatherland, Indonesia; One Nation, Indonesia; and, One Language, Bahasa Indonesia—the language of unity.

When the Japanese arrived in the 1940s, they also actively encouraged Bahasa Indonesia, using it to spread Japanese propaganda throughout the archipelago. Their efforts were very successful. Bahasa Indonesia became so widespread that after independence there was no question of changing the national language.

A welcome sign in an airport. The column on the left is in Bahasa Indonesia while the message is translated into English on the right.

The long history of contact between Indonesia and the rest of the world can be seen in the large number of Bahasa Indonesia words that have been borrowed from other languages. There are over 7,000 Dutch words (for example, *meubel* for furniture); Portuguese words (the island of Flores is Portuguese for flowers); English words (*doktor* and *bis* for doctor and bus); and numerous Sanskrit, Arabic, Polynesian, Tagalog, Chinese, French, Javanese, and Spanish words.

JAVANESE—THE LANGUAGE OF HIERARCHY

Imagine a language so complex that the words "to say" can be expressed in five ways: *kandha, sanjang, criyos, matur,* or *ngendika.* The word used depends on the "level" of speech chosen. And the level depends on the person speaking, to whom the words are addressed, their relative ages and status, the situation, sex, generation, the race of the speaker, and so on.

The three levels of Javanese speech are *Ngoko, Madya,* and *Krama*—each has different words for everyday things. *Ngoko* is the first language a child learns and is simple, unrefined, and used between close friends. The highest level is *Krama,* an elegant and polite speech used in formal situations. In between these is *Madya* speech, used when people of low status talk or when two close friends speak respectfully. In addition, there is low *Krama* and high *Krama* to indicate the status of the speakers, and other levels of speech used only for royalty and ritual feasts.

This complex, hierarchical language has been heavily influenced by the Indian caste system, where everyone must be addressed according to their rank. To use the wrong word would be insulting, and to speak on the wrong level can be socially disastrous. No wonder the Javanese find it easier to speak in Bahasa Indonesia!

BODY LANGUAGE

Indonesians are very reserved in their body movements and gestures. Unnecessarily flinging arms, jerking the head, and talking loudly (even in anger) is considered *kasar* ("KAH-sar") or unrefined. Sometimes, the implications of facial expressions, gestures, and other body signals say as much as, if not more than, the message in the words alone.

Here are some examples of body language peculiar to Indonesians:

THE HEAD AND THE FEET The head and the feet are, by virtue of their position, the most and least esteemed parts of the body respectively. The head contains the "life force" and is thus considered sacred. In the past, headhunters (like the Dayaks of Kalimantan and Torajanese of Sulawesi) would bring back enemy heads for good luck. Children should never be patted on the head. Respect is also shown by keeping one's head lower than the person being honored.

The Islamic "handshake."

Care must be taken with one's feet: pointing them at someone is disrespectful, and propping them up on a table is absolutely taboo.

GREETING In greetings there is no effusive hugging and kissing, just a respectful Islamic handshake. This is done by holding both the hands of the other person, then letting go and bringing your hands back to the chest. In social circles, however, the ladies kiss each other on both cheeks Dutch-style.

STANDING In most situations Indonesians stand with a humble and respectful posture: the hands lightly overlapped in front of the body and the head slightly bowed. When speaking to someone of higher status, Indonesians lower their eyes to show respect. Standing with the hands on the hips is aggressive, and holding them behind the back considered too superior.

WALKING When in a restricted space, one should ask permission before walking in front of someone. This is done by bending low, extending the right arm forward, mumbling a *permisi* ("per-MEE-see"), meaning please give me permission, or excuse me, then quickly walking across.

POINTING Indonesians only point with their thumb. Using any other finger is considered rude. The gesture is like a gentler version of that used in America for hitching a ride, but with a more open palm. This gesture is also used like a "go ahead" signal when asking someone to proceed. For instance, it is used to invite someone to begin eating by pointing at the food.

Pointing the Indonesian way to invite a guest to have a cup of coffee.

GESTURES Rude or obscene signs are seldom seen. One different gesture is the one indicating madness. Instead of circling the index finger at the ear, the hand is used in a sawing motion across the forehead.

SMILING Everyone smiles in Indonesia, but it does not always indicate happiness. The Javanese are known to giggle when they are sad, smile when they give bad news, and laugh when nervous or confused. This does not show amusement but indicates their belief that life should remain as calm and unruffled as possible.

ARTS

INDONESIA HAS A GREAT variety of folk and classical arts, all of which are an integral part of traditional life. Its shadow puppets and printed textiles are world-famous. Indonesian arts have been influenced by foreign cultures, especially ancient Indian and Chinese civilizations.

Two main types of traditional Indonesian art form are old Malay, which is the tradition in the remote interiors of Sumatra and Borneo; and the Javanese and Balinese art forms, which are influenced by the Hindu stories of the *Mahabharata* and *Ramayana*. Bali is of special cultural interest because its art traditions have remained untouched by Islam. Its art is heavily influenced by Hindu-Buddhist temple art, seen in the vegetal offerings and the beautifully stylized and symbolic palm leaf objects.

Above: **A Balinese dancer.**

Opposite: **The colorful wooden puppets used in** *wayang golek.*

The most sophisticated dance and art forms are found in Java, and for many centuries, were limited to the courts. The secrets of *gamelan* ("GAH-may-lahn") music, *wayang* ("WAH-young") drama, and the age-old *batik*-making ("BAH-tick") used to be strictly royal traditions. Until recently, these arts were practiced only by ladies of the nobility or by specially commissioned artists. The royal monopoly on classical dance, for instance, was not broken until 1918 when the first school was set up outside the palace walls.

MUSIC

Performed to accompany dance and drama, *gamelan* music is Indonesia's most important and historical musical art form; its roots can be traced back over 1,500 years. *Gamelan* music sounds marvelously fluid, something between jazz and the gentle rippling of water. Since it has no written score, the skills in playing *gamelan* have been passed down from generation to generation.

Today, *gamelan* accompanies dance, theater, and royal and religious festivities. It is even performed in mosques, but in keeping with Javanese *adat*.

There are two distinct versions of gamelan: the slow, stately, measured Javanese *gamelan* and the Balinese version that explodes with energy and vibrancy. A full *gamelan* orchestra has a combination of xylophones, drums, gongs, string instruments, and flutes. Depending on how important the occasion is, an orchestra can have between five and 80 instruments and musicians. Unlike most Western instruments, *gamelan* has a unique two-scale tuning method. This means every set has a distinctive sound based on the preference of the maker.

Drums are usually the most important instrument in a *gamelan*

An *angklung* orchestra.

orchestra, as they set the tempo. However, there can be regional differences in the musical instruments used: in western Java, the *angklung* ("AHNG-klong") is important, while in eastern Java a zither or string instrument is more popular. Central Java *gamelan* has a more elaborate form than western Java, and Balinese *gamelan* is the liveliest of all.

THE ANGKLUNG

The *angklung* is a simple portable instrument made from hollow bamboo tubes of various lengths suspended in a frame.

When the *angklung* frame is shaken, it produces a musical tinkling sound that is similar to the xylophone. In the olden days it was used to accompany armies marching into battle. It is especially popular in western Java today, though it is now used in *gamelan* orchestras and is played in school bands.

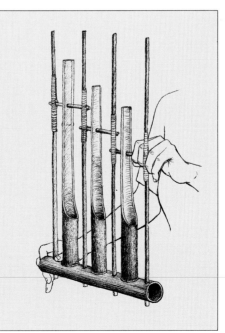

"There is something so extremely simple, and at the same time gay, in the sound produced by the rattling of these bamboo tubes, that I confess I have never heard the angklung *without pleasure."*

—Sir Stamford Raffles, *in* A History of Java.

93

DANCE

Indonesia's dance tradition is closely associated with rituals like exorcising spirits, performing rites of passage ceremonies such as birth, circumcision, and death, and celebrating various agricultural events. Both traditional or folk dances may be performed on these occasions. Besides entertainment, these dances also serve as important religious and cultural rituals.

Traditional and folk dances are vibrant, energetic, and require little formal training, but the famous classical dances of Java and Bali are quite the opposite. These dance traditions are heavily influenced by Indian cultural dance styles, as seen in the dance postures: bent knees, turned-out legs, straight body with head tilted to one side, and use of hand gestures.

Javanese classical dance is calm, controlled, and subtle. The dancer's eyes are always downcast, the limbs kept close to the body, and there are long, silent, hypnotizing pauses. On the other hand, Balinese dance is energetic. The dancers burst onto the stage, often to the sound of gongs

and cymbals, with eyes wide open and arms held high, often darting around in a manner that is totally different from the more refined Javanese version of classical dance.

The two main schools of Javanese dance are in Yogyakarta and Solo. Training starts when a child is 6 years old. It often takes years to perfect just one gesture, such as the arching of the fingers backward to touch the forearm.

Over 50 classical dances are performed in Java and Bali. Most are based on myth, religion, and the great Hindu epics of the *Ramayana* and *Mahabharata*. These dances are usually accompanied by *gamelan* orchestras.

Folk dances are performed all over Indonesia. Many of them are associated with important stages in a person's life or with agriculture, for example, dances to celebrate a good harvest season.

DRAMA AND PUPPETRY

Drama in Indonesia usually takes the form of puppetry. *Wayang,* as it is called, is more than a mere spectacle on stage and is probably the most powerful cultural force in the country. In depicting the stories of two great Indian epics, the *Ramayana* and the *Mahabharata, wayang* tells of the battle between good and evil, and also explores the strengths and weaknesses of people and society. *Wayang* (which means "shadow") is an ancient art form dating back to the 8th century when the epics were incorporated into drama to spread religion. It indirectly teaches about life and all its contradictions, imparts moral values, and provides heroic role models for the young.

Characters from the *wayang* are often used to describe personalities: an Arjuna is a good-looking, confident, and loyal person; Rawana embodies deception, evil, and greed; and Semar, one of the oldest and most respected characters, is an honorable name to give someone.

Wayang is so important to Indonesian cultural life that it is also used to spread government-sponsored statements to villages. Its performances are exciting, all-night affairs. When a traveling troupe arrives in a village, the entire community gathers to watch.

The ways of watching this type of theater are very different from Western theater. The atmosphere is noisy and informal where entire families—from grandmothers to young children—relax on mats on the floor and only half-watch the show; everyone is familiar with the ancient stories. *Wayang* watching is a relaxing event where people socialize, catch up on gossip, disappear to have something to eat, doze off when tired, and wake up when the gongs begin exciting battle scenes. All this continues into the early hours of the morning when everyone returns home, tired but happy, full of the wonderful stories of "brave heroes and great kingdoms."

A *wayang kulit* or shadow puppet.

Drama and Puppetry

The most popular types of drama are *wayang topéng* (masked drama), *wayang kulit* (shadow puppetry), *wayang golék* (wooden puppetry), and *wayang orang* (dance drama). Each of these is a regional specialty and tells of different stories and legends. Though *wayang kulit* and *wayang golék* are usually based on the Hindu epics, in central Java the *wayang golék* tells of popular folk legends based on the spread of Islam.

"There are those who watch the shadow play, weeping and sad in their foolish understanding, knowing full well that it is really only carved leather which moves and speaks."

—*11th century Javanese poem.*

In *wayang* performances, the puppeteer uses the puppets to enact the story and also acts as the narrator. *Wayang* performances are usually accompanied by a *gamelan* orchestra.

An intricate piece of antique *ikat* can cost thousands of dollars.

ARTS AND CRAFTS

Many of Indonesia's arts and crafts are world famous, especially its *ikat* and *batik* cloth, sculptures, and beautiful Balinese arts.

TEXTILES Indonesia has a wide range of traditional textiles, from primitive bark cloth, woven *ikat,* and silk *songket,* to sophisticated *batik.* These are believed to have ritualistic or religious significance. *Ikat* is used to swaddle the dead, *batik* is wrapped around a bridal couple to symbolize unity, and the *maa* ("mah") cloth of the Torajanese is used only for rituals.

Famous Indonesian textiles include the Sumatran "ship cloths," which depict a scene reminiscent of Noah's Ark with angular-armed people, plants, and animals. These are used to wrap a newborn child, and then for every successive significant event in that person's life, until finally the person dies and the cloth is buried with him or her.

Many of these traditional textiles take a great amount of time and effort to produce. *Ikat* ,which requires a traditional method of weaving threads together to create a design, can take up to 10 years to make. *Batik* production also requires an extraordinary amount of time and patience. This age-old art has been perfected by the Javanese, who produce the

finest *batik* in the world. The intricacy of this art is achieved with the hand-held *canting* ("CHAHN-ting"), which is used to draw fine wax patterns such as stylized human and animal figures on fabric. The cloth is dyed to color the non-waxed areas, the wax is washed off, and reapplied, and the entire process is repeated until the brilliant detail typical of *batik* is obtained. A cheaper and faster printing-block method is often used today.

Batik designs used to be deeply symbolic, with some reserved for royalty. Today, there are over 1,000 designs with 20 regional styles and countless color combinations.

WOOD SCULPTURE Indonesian wood carving ranges from the primitive tribal statues of Irian Jaya to intricate carvings in Java and Bali. Many of these have won international praise and can be found in art galleries.

JEWELRY Indonesia has a rich tradition in making gold and silver jewelry. The intricate silver jewelry from Bali and Yogyakarta is very popular. The more traditional jewelry includes the gold *mamuli* ("mah-moo-lee") pendants from Sumba and the bead necklaces of the Dayaks in Kalimantan.

BALI'S ART When people say, "Everyone in Bali is an artist," it is no exaggeration, as it appears that almost every Balinese has artistic talents. For its small size, Bali produces an amazing variety of paintings, sculpture, jewelry, weaving, and other crafts.

The Balinese have been avid painters for the last 400 years, and many have recently won international fame. Their original two- and three-dimensional paintings depict dozens of myths and stories simultaneously on the canvas. The island's sculptors produce everything from slim, elegant ebony rice-goddesses to fierce, bulging stone demons that guard all of Bali's crossroads and bridges.

So strong is the artistic atmosphere in Bali that many Western artists have settled there to draw inspiration from its people and culture.

THE MAGIC *KERIS*

The traditional handcrafted wavy-blade dagger is an important cultural symbol. It is not only a weapon but also a family's coat of arms.

It was once believed that a *keris* could possess a spirit and had magical powers to talk, walk, fly, and even kill a person by simply piercing his footprint. A *keris* could even warn of danger by rattling in its sheath, relieve a woman's labor pains, and avert floods.

The *keris* is also a ritual object used in religious and cultural ceremonies. If a groom is unable to be present at his marriage, he can still go through the marriage ceremony represented by his *keris*.

In past times, the *keris* was commonly worn by the Javanese upper class, and it is still worn on ceremonial occasions. It is believed to bring both good and bad luck so it is ceremoniously cleaned, wrapped in precious silks, and cared for by its owners.

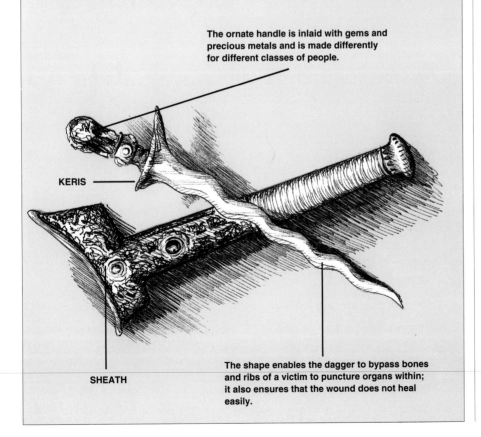

The ornate handle is inlaid with gems and precious metals and is made differently for different classes of people.

KERIS

SHEATH

The shape enables the dagger to bypass bones and ribs of a victim to puncture organs within; it also ensures that the wound does not heal easily.

LEISURE

WEEKENDS ARE IMPORTANT leisure times in Indonesia. People go shopping, visit neighbors and friends, catch up on gossip, and generally relax. Many go for a weekend jaunt to the countryside.

Many Jakartans leave the city and go to seaside resorts such as Anyer on Java's west coast, or take a boat out to the Thousand Islands, which is a pretty sprinkling of islands off the coast of Jakarta. Others prefer to leave the heat of the lowlands and go to the hill and mountain resorts. Bogor, Puncak, and Bandung are among the most popular cool weather stations with many of Jakarta's residents.

On the outskirts of Jakarta, another popular destination is the Ancol theme park, which provides entertainment for children and adults.

During celebrations and weekends in Jakarta, traffic is diverted from the main roads to make way for the hoards of residents who stream onto the empty streets for recreation. At daybreak, the streets start to fill with children and teenagers playing, dancing, or listening to music; skaters and cyclists; vendors—just about everyone joins in and enjoys the fun. Hawkers set up stalls selling food and the atmosphere becomes that of a street party.

In many villages, births, birthdays, weddings, and other life cycle events are accompanied by elaborate rituals and celebrations.

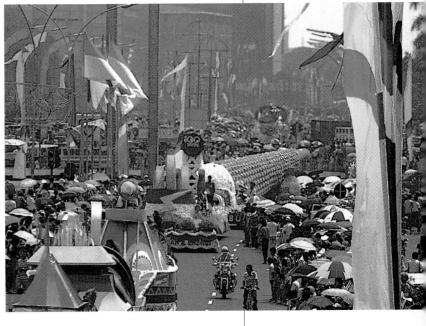

Above: **A parade to celebrate the anniversary of Jakarta's founding.**

Opposite: **A greased pole competition, a traditional game still enjoyed in Kalimantan.**

Right: **Owners preparing their birds for a cock fight.**

Below: **The dangerous sport of stone-jumping in Nias.**

TRADITIONAL GAMES AND SPORTS

There are numerous traditional games associated with the different islands of Indonesia.

In Nias, young men participate in the frightening sport of stone-jumping. The aim is to clear a thick stone wall about 5 feet high and 1.5 feet wide (1.5 m x 0.5 m), sometimes with a sword in hand. After running about 22 yards (20 m) up to the wall, the men jump high into the air, always landing feet first on the other side. These walls, once covered with sharp spikes, were used to train warriors to jump enemy walls while holding a torch in one hand and a sword in the other.

Indonesia is also a nation of seafarers and proud boat-makers: today, boat racing is a colorful tradition on several islands. Balinese men enjoy the sport of cock fighting, while the Madurese spend long hours preparing their sleek bulls for their annual bull races.

A demonstration of *pencak silat*, a form of martial arts.

Some sports are popular all over Indonesia. The sport of *sépak takraw*, which resembles volleyball, is an energetic game where two teams try to keep a plaited rattan ball in the air with their feet. A similar game is *sépak raga,* which is traditional to Sulawesi and Sumatra. Another sport, *pencak silat*, is a form of martial arts originating in Sumatra, where priests observed and copied the graceful yet lethal movements of animals. When it spread to the royal houses of Java, its deft movements were refined and perfected. Youths of both sexes train themselves in this art today.

Almost every Indonesian enjoys playing *congkak*, a game played with shells or pebbles placed in hollows on a wooden board. This game is especially popular at family gatherings.

MODERN GAMES AND SPORTS

The government's motto "Sports for All" aims to achieve a nation of sports-minded people. A National Sports Day is held every year on September 9, and participants from around the archipelago gather for a week of friendly competition in various sports.

The most popular sports are badminton and soccer. Indonesia is among the premier badminton-playing nations in the world and has won numerous international awards. Rudy Hartono is a living legend in Indonesia for winning the All-England badminton championship eight times. At the 1992 Olympic Games in Barcelona, Spain, the Indonesian duo of Susi Susanti and Alan Budikusuma made sports history when they each won a gold medal in the badminton singles final—the first ever gold medals won by Indonesia at the Olympic Games. Indonesia won one gold and two silver medals in the 2000 Sydney Olympics for badminton; and two silver and one bronze medal for weightlifting.

Boxing and tennis are also extremely popular sports. Indonesia's prize boxer, Ellyas Pical, has won international acclaim, while the nation's tennis team has brought home many regional trophies. Indonesia has also won international medals in table tennis.

FESTIVALS

INDONESIA HAS AN AMAZING array of festivals and celebrations throughout the year, both religious and cultural.

Bali has numerous colorful *odalan* ("oh-dahl-anh")—or temple anniversaries—religious holidays, and passage of life ceremonies that involve the whole community. On the island of Java, great traditional festivals are held by the royal courts on Islamic holidays. In other parts of Indonesia, there are harvest and sea festivals that are a mixture of local traditions and religious beliefs. Cities and towns also celebrate their anniversaries with sports events, traditional art performances, and elaborate processions.

Although Indonesia has official holidays, it is not easy to forecast the dates on which these holidays fall, since most of the dates are determined by different calendars. While the European calendar is based on the solar year of 365 days, the Muslim calendar is based on the lunar year of 354 days. Thus the dates of their festivals move back about 11 days every solar year. The Balinese and other ethnic groups calculate their calendars in other ways.

Since Indonesia is a Muslim country, most of its public holidays are Muslim festivals. Many of them are also more applicable to Java than to the other islands. But Indonesia also has a Hindu, Buddhist, and Christian population, and there is at least one public holiday for each of these communities.

Opposite: **Balinese women entering a temple gateway, their heads laden with offerings for a temple anniversary.**

PUBLIC HOLIDAYS

Jan. 1	New Year's Day
Jan. 30–31	Idul Fitri or Lebaran (end of Ramadan: period of Muslim fasting)
Mar./Apr.	Wafat Isa Al-Masih (Good Friday)
Mar. 26	Muharram (Islamic New Year)
Mar./Apr.	Nyepi (Hindu and Buddhist New Year)
Apr. 8	Idhul Adha (return of Muslim pilgrims from Mecca)
May 7	Waisak Day
Jun. 4	Garebeg (Prophet Mohammad's Birthday)
Aug. 17	Independence Day
Dec. 25	Christmas

ISLAMIC FESTIVALS

Lebaran (also called Idul Fitri) is the most important festival in Indonesia, marking the end of the fasting month observed by Muslims.

In the month before Lebaran (called Ramadan), Muslims fast from sunrise to sunset: children and adults alike do not eat or drink anything during daylight hours as a test of their spiritual values and self-discipline.

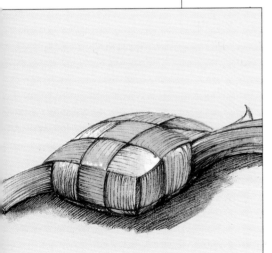

At the end of this fasting month, Lebaran is celebrated by noisy festivity throughout the Indonesian archipelago.

People wear new clothes, light firecrackers, prepare elaborate meals at home, and visit friends and relatives bearing gifts of specially prepared cakes and cookies. Streets are filled with people selling colorful cakes and the traditional *ketupat* ("ker-too-paht"), woven palm leaves stuffed with steamed rice.

Lebaran celebrations can last from a week to a whole month. At this time, young people also ask forgiveness from their elders for any wrongdoings committed during the year. The greeting *Selamat Idul Fitri: Ma'afkan Lahir Batin* ("Happy Idul Fitri and forgive us for all our wrongdoings") is heard in every home. This festival is also an occasion for paying respects to ancestors. Muslim Indonesians visit the family graves to pray and remember their deceased relatives.

Garebeg commemorates the birthday of the Prophet Mohammed and is marked by the biggest religious procession held in Java. Two days before Garebeg, large ceremonial food mounds are prepared at the royal palace during the Tumplak Wajik Festival. During Garebeg these mounds are taken in a procession to the main mosque of the city where they are blessed and distributed to waiting people. It is believed that getting a piece of the *gunungan* ("GOO-noong-ahn") or food mound will ensure good fortune and eternal youth, and also guarantee good harvests.

Isra Mi'raj Nabi Muhamad (the Ascension of the Prophet Mohammed) celebrates the night when the Archangel Gabriel took the Prophet Mohammed to heaven to speak with God.

Idul Adha is a sacrificial festival when cattle and goats are slaughtered to commemorate Ibrahim's (Abraham) willingness to sacrifice his firstborn son. At this time, Muslim pilgrims make the pilgrimage to Mecca. In Indonesia, family graves are also visited and cleaned during Idul Adha.

Hegira, the Islamic New Year, celebrates the day when the Prophet Mohammed made a trip from Mecca to start a new community in Medina, Saudi Arabia in A.D. 622.

Gunungan, or food mounds, being taken in a procession to the mosque during Garebeg.

Above: **The Nyepi festival is the biggest celebration on Hindu-dominated Bali.**

Opposite: **Offerings (top) and prayer and temple decorations (bottom) for the Balinese festival of Galungan.**

HINDU FESTIVALS

Hindu festivals are celebrated on the Hindu-dominated island of Bali. Nyepi, the Hindu New Year, is the most important. It is also called the Day of Complete Silence and is spent in prayer and meditation.

The eve of Nyepi, in contrast, is one of the noisiest days on the island. Offerings of wine and meat are laid out at every crossroads to appease the demons believed to reside there. Then as darkness falls, people come out to the streets beating loud gongs and cymbals, and bearing flaming torches

to chase away any remaining demons. Having chased away the evil spirits, everyone spends the next day in total silence, *nyepi* ("NEE-ah-pee"), to make sure that any returning demons will be tricked into believing that Bali is deserted and will go away. No fires are lit, no work or travel done, and no one leaves the home.

Galungan is another important Hindu festival in Bali, although it is not one of the official Indonesian holidays. During the 10 days of this festival, it is believed that the gods and revered ancestors return to earth. The Balinese spend long hours making intricate decorations and place these on pavements and at the entrances of temples and homes as offerings. Elaborate religious rituals take place in temples simultaneously throughout the island of Bali.

BUDDHIST FESTIVALS

Waisak, the most important festival for Buddhists, celebrates the three most significant moments of the life of Buddha, founder of the religion—his birth, his moment of enlightenment, and his death.

Thousands gather at the monumental 1,000-year-old Borobudur temple in central Java for this annual celebration. Here, a solemn procession of monks carrying flowers and reciting prayers winds its way around the terraces up to the main stupa in what is called the "Noble Silence." Offerings of fresh fruit and flowers are laid out at an ornately decorated altar.

The event climaxes when the moon is at its fullest. Thousands of devotees and monks light candles, meditate, and recite holy verses.

CHRISTIAN FESTIVALS

Christmas is celebrated in the traditional way among Christians in Indonesia, but Easter is celebrated in an unusual way on the island of Flores.

Wearing dark clothes, triangular white hoods, and costumes reminiscent of 16th-century Portugal, Christians make a barefoot procession through the streets of Flores at midnight. A statue of the Virgin Mary that is said to have washed ashore many years ago and a symbolic black coffin of Jesus are carried along to the beat of muffled drums. With marchers carrying torches and candles and waving grass pom-poms in the air, the procession is an eerie, though fascinating, event to watch.

The midnight Easter procession on the predominantly Christian island of Flores.

The Bull Races of Madura are held every year during August or September. In the past plow teams raced the length of a rice field, but today, racing bulls are specially bred for this race. Winning this race brings great prestige and is a source of regional pride.

OTHER FESTIVALS

With the diversity of cultural life in Indonesia's thousands of islands, festivals and celebrations are held all over the country.

The Bull Races of Madura are a colorful and exciting event that takes place after the harvest season. The bulls raced are fed a diet of chili peppers, honey, beer, and raw eggs. On the day of the race, they are brilliantly dressed and paraded through town. Once they reach the stadium, they are raced at speeds of over 30 miles (48 km) per hour down the 110-yard (100-m) track with their jockeys perched behind on wooden sleds. Finally, the victorious bull is proudly trotted home to be used as a stud.

The Kesodo Festival is held at Bromo volcano in east Java. Every year, thousands of mountain-dwelling Tenggerese people from the surrounding countryside make a 14-day pilgrimage to Bromo. At a midnight ceremony on the 15th day, they offer sacrifices of flowers, rice, chickens, and goats to the goddess of Bromo volcano. According to legend, the first ancestor

of the Tenggerese sacrificed his 25th child to the volcano goddess in return for abundant crops and many children. Today, those who make the pilgrimage to Bromo ask for protection from volcanic eruptions and for good harvests in the coming year.

Kartini Day honors Raden Ajeng Kartini (1879-1904), Indonesia's first woman liberator and one of its most honored national heroes. In her time, Kartini spoke up not only against the restrictive Javanese *adat* (custom) system but also for women's right to education.

On this commemorative day, parades, lectures, and school activities are held in her honor. They are attended by women throughout Indonesia, wearing their different regional dresses to symbolize the unity of the nation's women. Also, as on Mother's Day in the West, women are not allowed to work at home—children and fathers take over household chores.

The annual Independence Day is celebrated with processions, dancing, and parades. Starting on August 17, festivities can last up to a month.

FOOD

AT THE CROSSROADS of the ancient trade routes, Indonesia's cuisine has been shaped by an incredible mixture of foreign influences. From India came curries and turmeric, from the Chinese stir-frying and the indispensable *wok,* and from the Arabs it was *kebab* and other mutton dishes. The Dutch introduced vegetables such as the carrot, tomato, pumpkin, and cauliflower. The Japanese and Thai immigrant cultures have also added variety to Indonesian cuisine.

Surprisingly, the traditional spices such as nutmeg, pepper, mace, and cloves for which Indonesia is famous are not commonly used in Indonesian cuisine. Instead, the delicate flavor of fresh herbs such as lemon grass, candlenut, and basil are more popular.

Indonesia is home to many tropical fruits, including watermelons, guavas, mangoes, papayas, a variety of bananas, starfruit, avocadoes, *duku* ("DOO-koo"), rambutan, and durian. The duku grows in clusters like bunches of large buff-coloured grapes with a thin skin. Inside are five segments of juicy white flesh.

There is also a local remedy for everything from ageing to impotence to good skin and weight-loss. Called *jamu,* it is commercially produced in Javanese factories from a blend of herbs, minerals, grasses, roots, barks, parts of mammals, birds, reptiles, and jungle plants.

Above: **A merchant displaying his wares of onions, garlic, crackers and chips.**

Opposite: **A typical market scene in the remoter parts of Indonesia, where produce is displayed on the ground.**

One of Indonesia's most famous dishes is sate, where skewered strips of meat are barbequed over a charcoal fire and served with a peanut sauce, chopped cucumbers, and onions.

FAVORITE FOODS

Rice is the staple food in most parts of Indonesia and can be eaten for breakfast, lunch, and dinner with either fish, meat, vegetables, or eggs. The popular *nasi goreng* ("nah-see GOH-raeng"), or fried rice, is a very popular rice dish. Many snacks and sweet dishes are also made with rice. In the eastern islands of Indonesia, the staple foods are corn, sago, cassava, and sweet potatoes.

Fish and other seafood are also important food sources in Indonesia. Other favorites are *tahu* ("TAH-hoo"), or soybean cake, and fermented soy beans wrapped in banana leaf called *tempe* ("TAME-pay"). These are inexpensive and so rich in protein that they are called the vegetarian meat of the poor. Poultry and eggs are more commonly eaten than red meat.

Coconut is an important ingredient in most Indonesian dishes, adding richness to curries and sauces. Another favorite is a spicy peanut sauce that is poured over salads and accompanies the traditional *sate* ("SAH-tay")— pieces of meat seasoned with spices and grilled on bamboo skewers.

Indonesians also make dishes from unusual parts of edible plants such as leaves from bamboo, mango, papaya, cassava, and cashew nut trees, and flowers from the hibiscus plant, banana tree, plus a variety of nuts and seeds.

Most Indonesian food is highly spiced with hot chili peppers or is accompanied by a fiery red chili paste called *sambal* ("SAHM-baal"). The preparation of *sambal* is such an important part of Indonesian cooking that the cooking skill of young girls is judged according to the quality of *sambal* that they prepare.

Other popular Indonesian dishes are *gado-gado* ("gah-doh gah-doh"), a vegetable salad served with a peanut sauce, and *bakmi goreng* ("buk-mee GOH-rayng") or fried noodles.

Intricate images made of rice are used in many cultural ceremonies and are considered works of art.

RICE—THE SYMBOL OF LIFE

Rice is not just the staple food of Indonesia but is also symbolic of life itself. Images of the rice goddess are found everywhere.

From planting to harvest time, the rice crop is carefully nurtured. It is believed that any carelessness will chase away the sacred soul of rice, Dewi Sri, and result in crop failure.

During harvest time, care is taken to respect the soul of rice. Harvesters hide their cutting blade in their hand and murmur apologies to Dewi Sri while they cut the rice stalks.

Many of Indonesia's fertility rites involve rice as the symbol of life and continuity. Inverted cones of colored rice are essential for many ceremonies. During major religious festivals, decorated mounds of rice are distributed and either eaten or left in the fields to ensure a plentiful harvest.

So important is rice to Indonesia's lifestyle that a university professor's salary even includes a 10-pound sack of rice!

DRINKS AND DESSERTS

Indonesian beverages are colorful drinks that are often served also as desserts. Among the favorites are creamy fresh avocado juice, sweet perfumed Java tea, and thick black *kopi tubruk* ("KOH-pee toh-BROOK" meaning collision coffee, which is prepared by pouring boiling water onto coffee grounds). A refreshing drink is coconut juice drunk straight from a young coconut with its top sliced off. Locally brewed alcoholic drinks are drunk by non-Muslim Indonesians. These include *tuak* ("TOO-ahk"), or palm wine; *brem* ("braem"), which is brewed from rice and coconut milk; and *bedek* ("bay-DAYK"), or rice wine.

ES TELER, THE KING OF DRINKS

Es Teler is a popular drink and dessert. A typical version is made as follows:

Ingredients
$^3/_4$ glass ice water
2 teaspoons sugar syrup
2 drops vanilla flavoring
chopped avocado pieces
coconut shavings
chopped colored gelatin
chopped jackfruit

Method
Mix all the ingredients together. Chill for two hours and serve.

TROPICAL FRUIT

There is an amazing array of tropical fruit in Indonesia. Besides the common bananas and pineapples, Indonesia has some unusual produce.

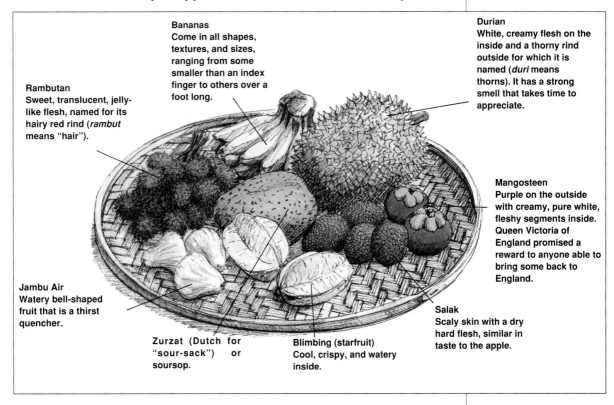

Bananas
Come in all shapes, textures, and sizes, ranging from some smaller than an index finger to others over a foot long.

Durian
White, creamy flesh on the inside and a thorny rind outside for which it is named (*duri* means thorns). It has a strong smell that takes time to appreciate.

Rambutan
Sweet, translucent, jelly-like flesh, named for its hairy red rind (*rambut* means "hair").

Mangosteen
Purple on the outside with creamy, pure white, fleshy segments inside. Queen Victoria of England promised a reward to anyone able to bring some back to England.

Jambu Air
Watery bell-shaped fruit that is a thirst quencher.

Salak
Scaly skin with a dry hard flesh, similar in taste to the apple.

Zurzat (Dutch for "sour-sack") or soursop.

Blimbing (starfruit)
Cool, crispy, and watery inside.

Above: **A Bugis feast. The food is placed in the middle and the diners help themselves from a choice of dishes.**

TABLE MANNERS

Indonesians are very hospitable people and always invite others present to join them before starting a meal. To eat without giving a thought to others is considered most uncivilized. Guests are always honored with special treatment. If they are present, the table is laden with far more food than guests can possibly eat.

All the dishes are brought to the table together. Everyone takes a mound of rice on his or her plate and then tries the other dishes with the rice. In rural areas, the food is placed on a large woven mat in the center of the kitchen with everyone sitting cross-legged around it.

The traditional way to eat is with the fingers of the right hand. Indonesians believe that food tastes better when it is eaten by hand rather than with a fork and spoon. They only use their right hand to eat as the

left hand is considered unclean. Likewise, food should be served and passed with the right hand. Some servants may also bow or stoop as they serve guests as a sign of respect.

In the cities and towns, people do use a fork and spoon. Knives are not necessary since the food is usually cut up into small pieces. But the rural folk still do eat with their fingers.

Visitors should learn to wait patiently until invited to eat or drink by the host. It is also polite not to finish everything on your plate; if you do, it means you are not satisfied and want more.

A host and guest eating with their fingers on the front porch of a house in Sumba.

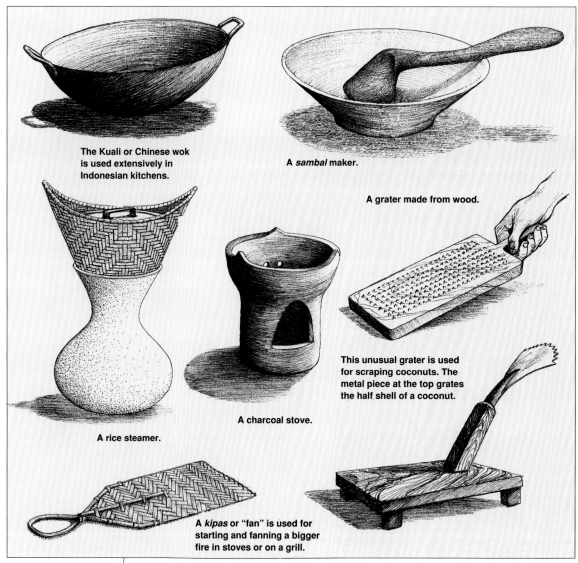

The Kuali or Chinese wok is used extensively in Indonesian kitchens.

A *sambal* maker.

A grater made from wood.

This unusual grater is used for scraping coconuts. The metal piece at the top grates the half shell of a coconut.

A charcoal stove.

A rice steamer.

A *kipas* or "fan" is used for starting and fanning a bigger fire in stoves or on a grill.

KITCHEN UTENSILS

Many kitchen utensils used are particular to Indonesia. Half a coconut shell attached to a split bamboo handle is used as a ladle. The simple wooden mortar and pestle is specially designed to grind the popular *sambal*.

Almost all kitchens have a rice steamer, a special conical steamer made from strips of split bamboo that allows steam from the boiling water below to pass through the rice and cook it.

FOOD PREFERENCES AND TABOOS

Each province or region has different types of food. Javanese food consists of vegetables, soybeans, beef, and chicken, while in the eastern islands, seafood is more important. The Sumatrans eat more beef, while in Bali, Irian Jaya, and northern Sulawesi, pork is more popular. The Muslim population does not eat pork as it is considered unclean, and they also avoid alcohol.

In some regions, some unusual dishes can include dog meat, mice, eels, and roasted lizards. Other regional delicacies include *tretis* ("TRAY-tis"), or partially digested grass from a cow's stomach, dried pork and chicken blood, fried animal skins, and intestines and offal.

A *Jamu* girl with her products walking along a Jakarta street. Interested buyers can stop her in the street and buy jamu on the spot.

HEALING POWERS OF JAMU

Traditional herbal remedies, called *jamu*, are very popular with Indonesians. These pastes, powders, creams, and capsules are consumed daily and used to cure everything from headaches and fatigue to leprosy and flabby stomachs.

These fascinating natural remedies originated in the royal courts of Yogyakarta and Solo. There, the ladies of the nobility spent their time discovering and perfecting the science of using roots, flowers, barks, nuts, herbs, and spices to retain their beauty and vigor.

Today, these ancient ancestral recipes are used to commercially manufacture a wide variety of *jamu* for Indonesians who are firmly convinced of their curative powers.

Right: **Customers gather at the nearby warung to eat, drink, and exchange news.**

Below: **A kaki lima vendor.**

EATING OUT

Eating out is a popular pastime. Indonesians often stop a *kaki lima* ("kah-kee LEE-mah") vendor to have a meal on the spot, visit a roadside *warung* ("WAH-roong"), squat on mats on the street for traditional *gudeg* ("gooh-dayg"), or choose from a table laden with dishes in a Padang restaurant.

THE KAKI LIMA   Named after the 5-feet-wide (1.5-m-wide) sidewalks in Indonesia, *kaki lima* (literally "five-foot way") are food vendors plying these sidewalks. They carry all their food and cooking utensils in two cabinets hanging from upward curving bamboo yokes. These colorful vendors have become an institution as Indonesia's walking restaurants, each having a characteristic cry or sound to attract customers, from a rattle of brass bells to the beating of a Chinese wooden block. When summoned, the vendor lowers his wares, squats in front of you, fans his charcoal brazier to a glow, and quickly cooks a dozen sticks of *sate* or a bowl of noodles on the spot.

MALIOBORO—THE LONGEST RESTAURANT IN THE WORLD

Jalan Malioboro in Yogyakarta is famous for having possibly the longest restaurant in the world. It is actually one of the main roads in this city, where every evening vendors line its pavements with bamboo mats and set up food stalls. Customers sit cross-legged on these mats to enjoy traditional *gudeg* (chicken cooked in jackfruit) and drink clear, sweet tea until the early hours of the morning.

A warung.

WARUNG A *warung* is the closest Indonesian equivalent to a snack bar. Customers gather to have a drink, order a quick meal cooked on the spot, nibble on snacks, exchange news, or just while away some time. All a *warung* needs is a roof, a table, a counter to display jars of brightly-colored snacks, and a bench for seating.

PADANG FOOD Sumatran food from Padang is famous for the variety and number of dishes. In a typical meal, the table is laden with a feast of 10 to 25 dishes, and diners can pick and choose what they want.

FERMENTED SOYBEAN AND GREEN BEANS IN COCONUT MILK (*TUMIS TEMPE SANTAN KECAP*)

Tempe is fermented soybean. It can be substituted in recipes calling for meat, poultry, or fish. Cook it with soy sauce or lightly salted water to aid digestion. High in protein, fiber, iron, and calcium, it is also low in saturated fats. Instead, it contains essential fats such as Omega 3 oils, which help to distribute the fat-soluble vitamins around the bloodstream and supply energy to the body.

Ingredients:
3 tablespoons oil
10 oz. (300 g) fermented soybean
7 shallots (finely sliced)
3 cloves of garlic (finely sliced)
5 green chilies (sliced into 0.4 inch/1 cm pieces)
2 red chilies (sliced into 0.4 inch/1 cm pieces)
1 salam leaf (or bay leaf as a substitute)
0.4 inch/1 cm ginger root (bruised)
2 tomatoes (each cut into 4–6 pieces)
2 cups (500 cc) coconut milk
3 tablespoons sweet soy sauce
1 teaspoon salt
2 teaspoons brown sugar
15 green beans (halved)
6 oz. (200 g) shrimp

Cut fermented soybean into 0.4 inch/1 cm cubes. Fry until half-cooked then drain. Sauté shallots and garlic until fragrant. Add chilies, salam leaf, ginger root, and tomatoes. Stir until the ingredients are soft. Then add fermented soybean, coconut milk, sweet soy sauce, salt, and sugar. Add green beans and shrimp. Simmer until the sauce has thickened.

MIXED VEGETABLE SALAD WITH PEANUT SAUCE (*GADO-GADO*)

Gado-gado is a staple vegetarian dish throughout the country. It is easy to make, healthy, and delicious.

Ingredients:
2 oz. (60 g) bean sprouts
(tailed, blanched, drained)
5 oz. (150 g) spinach leaves
(boiled, drained)
6 oz. (200 g) bitter gourd
(seeded, sliced, boiled)
1 3 x 3 inch (8 x 8 cm) piece of bean
curd (fried, sliced)
1 3 x 3 inch (8 x 8 cm) piece of
fermented soybean (fried, sliced)
3 hard-boiled eggs (sliced)
1–2 tablespoons of fried shallots
prawn crackers

You may also use other vegetables in season, such as sliced carrots, string beans, white cabbage, and broccoli.

Peanut sauce:
6 oz. (200 g) peanuts
   (fried, skin removed, ground)
2 red chilies
   (ground)
1 teaspoon salt
   (ground)
1/2 tablespoon brown sugar 0.8 cups (200 cc)
   water/coconut milk

Mix the peanut sauce ingredients and bring to the boil. Pour peanut sauce over vegetables, fried bean curd, and fermented soybean in a bowl. Garnish with egg slices, a sprinkle of fried shallots, and crushed prawn crackers.

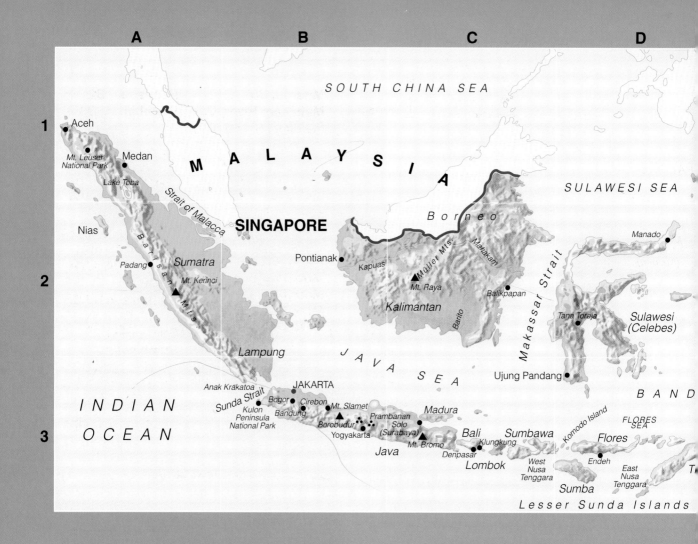

MAP OF INDONESIA

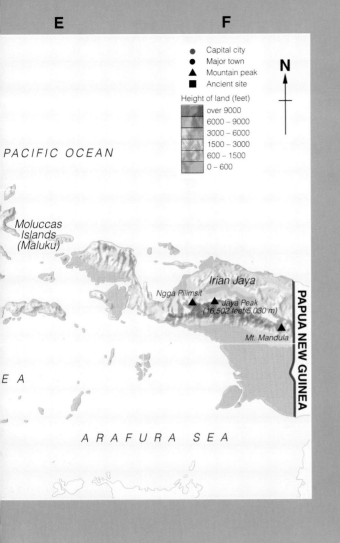

E   F

- ● Capital city
- ● Major town
- ▲ Mountain peak
- ■ Ancient site

Height of land (feet)

	over 9000
	6000 – 9000
	3000 – 6000
	1500 – 3000
	600 – 1500
	0 – 600

N

PACIFIC OCEAN

Moluccas
Islands
(Maluku)

Irian Jaya

Ngga Pilimsit

Jaya Peak
(16,502 feet/5,030 m)

Mt. Mandula

PAPUA NEW GUINEA

E A

ARAFURA SEA

Madura, C3
Mahakam River, C2
Makassar Strait, C2,
  C3, D2
Malaysia, A1, A2,
  B1, B2, C1, C2
Moluccas Islands
  (Maluku), E2
Manado, D2
Medan, A1
Mount Bromo, C3
Mount Kerinci, A2
Mount Jaya, F2
Mount Leuser
  Nat-ional Park,
  A1
Mount Mandula,
  F2
Mount Raya, C2
Mount Slamet, B3
Muller Mountains,
  C2

Ngga Pilimsit, F2
Nias, A2

Padang, A2
Papua New Guinea,
  F2, F3

Pontianak, B2
Prambanan, B3

Singapore, B2
South China Sea,
  A1, B1, B2, C1
Strait of Malacca,
  A1, A2, B2
Sulawesi (Celebes),
  C2, D2, D3
Sulawesi Sea, D1,
  D2
Sumatra, A1, A2,
  B2, B3
Sumba, D3
Sumbawa, C3
Sunda Strait, B3
Solo (Surabaya), C3

Tana Toraja, D2
Timor, D3, E3

Ujung Pandang, D3

West Nusa
  Tenggara, C3

Yogyakarta, B3

Flores Trench, D3

Indian Ocean, A1,
  A2, A3, B3, C3,
  D3
Irian Jaya, E2, F2, F3

Jakarta, B3
Java, B3, C3
Java Sea, B2, B3, C2,
  C3
Jaya Peak, F2

Kalimantan, B2, C1,
  C2
Kapuas River, B2,
  C2
Klungkung, C3
Komodo Island, D3
Kulon Peninsula
  National Park, B3

Lake Toba, A1
Lampung, B2, B3
Lombok, C3

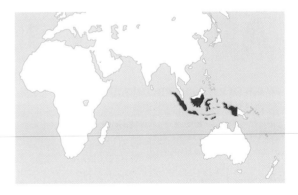

ECONOMIC INDONESIA

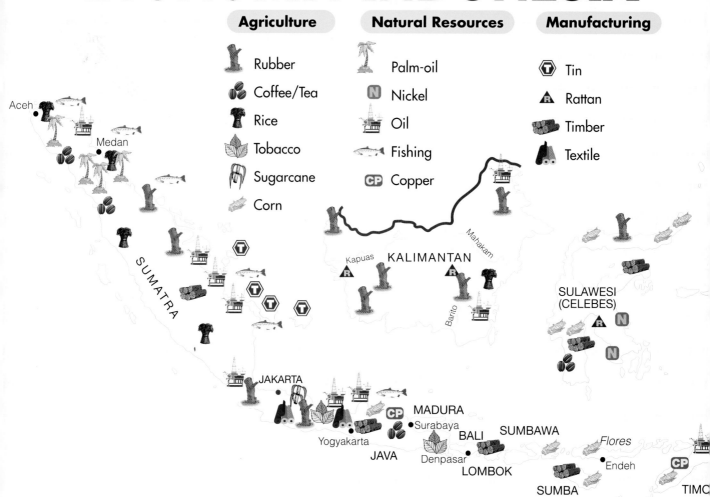

Agriculture
- Rubber
- Coffee/Tea
- Rice
- Tobacco
- Sugarcane
- Corn

Natural Resources
- Palm-oil
- N Nickel
- Oil
- Fishing
- CP Copper

Manufacturing
- T Tin
- R Rattan
- Timber
- Textile

Aceh
Medan
SUMATRA
Kapuas
KALIMANTAN
Mahakam
Barito
SULAWESI (CELEBES)
JAKARTA
MADURA
Surabaya
Yogyakarta
JAVA
Denpasar
BALI
LOMBOK
SUMBAWA
Flores
Endeh
SUMBA
TIMO

ABOUT THE ECONOMY

GROSS DOMESTIC PRODUCT
US$610 billion (1999 estimate)

NATURAL RESOURCES
Petroleum, tin, natural gas, nickel, timber, bauxite, copper, fertile soils, coal, gold, silver.

GDP REAL GROWTH RATE
4–5 percent (2001 estimate)

GDP COMPOSITION BY SECTOR
Services: 44 percent (1999 estimates)
Industry: 35 percent (1999 estimates)
Agriculture: 21 percent (1999 estimates)

MOLUCCAS
ISLANDS
(MALUKU)

IRIAN JAYA

AGRICULTURAL PRODUCTS
Rice, cassava (tapioca), peanuts, rubber,
cocoa, coffee, palm oil, copra; poultry, beef,
pork, eggs.

INFLATION RATE (CONSUMER PRICES)
10.5 percent (2001 estimate)

WORK FORCE
88 million (1998 estimate)

UNEMPLOYMENT RATE
15–20 percent (1998 estimate)

MAJOR EXPORTS
Oil accounts for about 30 percent of export earnings.
Liquified Natural Gas (LNG) is the second largest
earner of foreign exchange. Other exports:
machinery, chemicals, foodstuffs, agricultural
products, iron and steel products, textiles and
clothing, seafood, timber, rubber, and coffee. Its
major export partners: Japan 18 percent, EU 15
percent, US 14 percent, Singapore 13 percent,
South Korea 5 percent, Hong Kong 4 percent,
China 4 percent, Taiwan 3 percent (1999 estimate).

MAJOR IMPORTS
Indonesia produces cars, electrical components,
and clothing. Its imports are therefore largely
restricted to capital equipment, chemical and oil
products, base metal, beverages, and luxury
Western items for the well-to-do. Its main
import partners: Japan 17 percent, US 13 percent,
Singapore 10 percent, Germany 9 percent,
Australia 6 percent, South Korea 5 percent, Taiwan
3 percent, China 3 percent (1999 estimate).

PORTS AND HARBORS
Cilacap, Cirebon, Jakarta, Kupang, Palembang,
Semarang, Surabaya, Ujung Pandang.

AIRPORTS
446

RAILWAYS
4,013 miles (about 6,458 km)

HIGHWAYS
212,944 miles (342,700 km)

WATERWAYS
13,409 miles (about 21,580 km)

CURRENCY
Indonesian rupiah (Rp) = 100 sen
US$1 = 11,421.00 Rp (May 23, 2001)

CULTURAL INDONESIA

Aceh

Medan

DIENG PLATEAU
The Dieng Plateau in Java presents an extraordinary landscape: a rich volcanic basin of sulphur springs, lakes, and Hindu temples which are some of Indonesia's oldest remains, dating from the 6th century. Eight (out of a possible 200) small temples remain, originally dedicated to Siva, the Hindu god of destruction.

MADURA
Madura Island is remarkable for the range and style of its traditional sailing vessels, which have a distinctive boomed triangular sail (called a protolateen rig). Such vessels include the *prahu jaring*, *golekan*, *lis-alis*, *leti leti*, and *janggolan*.

TORAJA FUNERALS (Tana Toraja, Sulawesi)
The Toraja are famous for their elaborate funerals, which involve vast numbers of guests, sacrifices of buffaloes, dances, parades and great feasts. Carved life-sized wooden effigies of the dead (*tau tau*) are then set on stone galleries carved out of the cliffs.

K A L I M A N T A N

SULAWESI (CELEBES)

NIAS
Nias contains a Stone Age civilization which is famous for their woodcarving, dances, and stone-jumping. Stone pedestals, called *hombo batu*, usually about 7 feet (about 2 m) high, were traditionally vaulted by warriors in preparation for battle.

JAKARTA

MINANGKABAU HOUSES
The matrilineal Minangkabau of West Sumatra are famous for their wooden houses (*rumah gadang*) with curved roofs which look like buffalo horns. Raised 3–7 feet (1–2 m) off the ground on stilts, the walls are elaborately carved and painted with plant and animal motifs.

TAMAN MINI
Taman Mini, in the southeast of Jakarta replicates the whole country in one park. Opened in 1975, its 0.5-square-mile (1.2-square-km) site contains 27 full-scale traditional houses from each of Indonesia's provinces and also displays regional handicrafts and cultural performances.

Borobudur

Yogyakarta

BOROBUDUR
Borobudur ranks with Cambodia's Angkor Wat as one of the greatest Buddhist monuments in Southeast Asia. Almost 78,477 cubic yards (60,000 cubic m) and consisting of a 9-tiered "mountain" rising to 113.2 feet (34.5 m), Borobudur is made from 1.6 million andesite stones and decorated with some 1,500 reliefs and 500 statues of the Buddha.

Solo (Surabaya)

PRAMBANAN PLAIN
These magnificent temples are second only to Borobudur in splendor. Candi Prambanan is the greatest Hindi monument in Java. Its central tower is over 148 feet (45 m) tall and originally consisted of 232 temples. Its three largest candis were dedicated to Brahma, Vishnu, and Siva.

MADURA

BALI

SUMBAWA

Flores

JAVA

LOMBOK

SUMBA

TIM

BALI DANCES
The Balinese are prodigious dancers. There are daily dance performances on the island. An essential part of private and public life, the best known dances are the masked dance (*topeng*), the monkey dance (*kecak*), and the dance between the witch Rangda and the mythical lion (*barong*).

IKAT WEAVING
Ikat, or resist dyeing, is a techni of cloth patterning found all ove Indonesia. Either the warp or th weft is tied with material or fibe resist the action of the dye. Dou ikat, however, where both the w and weft are tie-dyed, is produc in only one place in Southeast Asi the village of Tenganan in East B

ABOUT THE CULTURE

OFFICIAL NAME
Indonesia

CAPITAL
Jakarta

SYSTEM OF GOVERNMENT
Republic. Current chief of state: President Abdurrahman Wahid of the National Awakening Party; Vice president: Megawati Sukarnoputri of the Indonesian Democratic Party-Struggle.

MOLUCCAS
ISLANDS
MALUKU

IRIAN JAYA

ETHNIC GROUPS
Ethnic groups: Javanese 45 percent, Sundanese 14 percent, Madurese 7.5 percent, coastal Malays 7.5 percent, others 26 percent.

RELIGIONS
Muslim 88 percent, Protestant 5 percent, Roman Catholic 3 percent, Hindu 2 percent, Buddhist 1 percent, others 1 percent.

LANGUAGES & DIALECTS
Bahasa Indonesia (official, modified form of Malay), English, Dutch, local dialects, the most widely spoken of which is Javanese.

LITERACY
84.9% (1997 estimate)

LIFE EXPECTANCY
64.8 years (1997 estimate)

NATIONAL ANTHEM
Indonesia Raya (Great Indonesia)

HOLIDAYS & FESTIVALS
New Year's Day, Lebaran, Wafat Isa Al-Masih, Muharram, Nyepi, Idhul Adha, Waisak Day, Garebeg, Independence Day, Christmas.

DESCRIPTION OF FLAG
Two equal horizontal bands of red (top) and white.

POPULATION
224,784,210 (July 2000 estimate)

POLITICAL PARTIES
National Awakening Party (PKB); Indonesia Democracy Party-Struggle (PDI-P); Joint Secretariat of Functional Groups (Golkar); Development Unity Party (PPP); Indonesia Democracy Party (PDI); National Mandate Party (PAN). (Since the 1999 general election.)

TIME LINE

IN INDONESIA	IN THE WORLD
	753 B.C. Rome founded.
	116–17 B.C. Roman Empire reaches its greatest extent, under Emperor Trajan (98–17 B.C.).
A.D. 600–700 Srivijaya Kingdom founded.	**600** Height of Mayan civilization.
778–850 Borobudur is constructed.	
	1000 Chinese perfect gunpowder and begin to use it in warfare.
1294 Majapahit Kingdom is founded.	
End of 13th century Islam introduced to Indonesia.	
14th century Majapahit Kingdom goes into decline and invaded by new Islamic state of Demak.	
1510s Portuguese take control of Maluku.	
	1530 Beginning of trans-Atlantic slave trade organized by Portuguese in Africa.
	1558–1603 Reign of Elizabeth I of England.
	1620 Pilgrim Fathers sail the Mayflower to America.
1700s Indonesia comes under the control of the Dutch.	

IN INDONESIA	IN THE WORLD
	1776 US Declaration of Independence.
	1789–1799 The French Revolution.
1811 Java falls to the British East India Company.	
1815–1920 Dutch regains rule over Indonesia.	**1861** US Civil War begins.
	1869 The Suez Canal is opened
1908 Formation of Budi Utomo ("High Endeavor") marks the start of organized nationalism.	**1914** World War I begins
	1939 World War II begins
1945 Proclamation of the independent Republic of Indonesia with Sukarno as its first president.	**1945** The United States drops atomic bombs on Hiroshima and Nagasaki
1966 Suharto seizes power from Sukarno after a military coup and is appointed president in 1968.	**1966–1969** Chinese Cultural Revolution
1999 Abdurrahman Wahid declared president and Megawati Sukarnoputri vice president. Referendum in East Timor rejects Indonesian rule.	**1991** Break-up of Soviet Union
2001 Violence in East Timor continues.	**2001** World population surpasses 6 billion

GLOSSARY

adat ("AAH-dut")—Customs, traditions, and culture of a people.

Allabo-akbar ("ehl-LAH ho-EHK-behr")—The Muslim muezzin's call to prayer which means "God is great."

animism—Belief that all natural objects (rocks, trees, etc.) possess souls.

babasa ("bah-HAH-sah")—Language. Bahasa Indonesia is Indonesia's national language.

batik ("BAH-tick")—Indonesian textile on which patterns are drawn in wax then dyed in colors.

Bhinneka Tunggal Ika ("bhee-nay-kah toong-gahl ee-kah")—Unity in Diversity, the national motto.

gamelan ("GAH-may-lahn")—An Indonesian orchestra playing traditional music.

gotong royong ("goh-TOHNG roh-YOHNG")—A concept meaning cooperation or working together as a community.

jamu ("JAR-moo")—Traditional herbal tonic.

kasar ("KAH-sar")—unrefined behavior, e.g. flailing of arms or speaking in a loud voice.

keris ("KER-is")—A dagger with a wavy blade.

ladang ("LAH-dahng")—"Slash and burn" agricultural technique.

mandi ("MAHN-dee")—A large stone basin where water is stored for bathing.

mufakat ("moo-FAH-kaht")—Discussion

Salam alaikum ("ehs seh-LAHM eh-lei-koom")—A Muslim greeting meaning "Peace be unto you."

sambal ("SAHM-baal")—Spicy sauce made from ground chilies and served with rice.

sarung ("SAH-roong")—An ankle-length cloth or skirt worn by both men and women, usually with block patterns.

saudara ("sah-hu-DAH-rah")—A term of address meaning relative of the same generation.

seléndang ("SER-land-dung")—A long, narrow piece of batik, used as a shawl or a sling.

stupa—Dome enclosing an effigy of Buddha.

wayang ("WAH-young")—Shadow play with leather or flat wooden puppets, usually dramatizing themes from Hindu epics.

FURTHER INFORMATION

BOOKS

Dalton, Bill. *Indonesia Handbook*. California: Moon Publications, 1995.

Turner, Peter, et al. *Lonely Planet Indonesia*. London: Lonely Planet Publications, 2000.

Von Holzen, Heinz, et al. *The Food of Indonesia: Authentic Recipes from the Spice Islands*. California: Periplus Editions, 1999.

Whitten, Tony, et al. *The Ecology of Java and Bali* (*Ecology of Indonesia Series*, Volume 2). Kuala Lumpur: OUP, 1997.

WEBSITES

Central Intelligence Agency World Factbook (select Indonesia from the country list).
   www.odci.gov/cia/publications/factbook/index.html

Essays on Indonesian politics and economics. www.laksamana.net

The Indonesian Yellow Pages 2001. www.yellowpages.co.id

International Monetary Fund website. www.imf.org/external/country/IDN/index.htm

Learn2.com language learning. www.learn2.com/08/0828/0828.html

Learning Network reference (type "Indonesia" in the search box). http://ln.infoplease.com

Lonely Planet World Guide: Destination Indonesia.
   www.lonelyplanet.com/destinations/south_east_asia/indonesia/

The World Bank Group (type "Indonesia" in the search box). www.worldbank.org

Worldskip.com tourist information. www.worldskip.com/indonesia

The World-Wide Web Virtual Library: Indonesia.
   www.coombs.anu.edu.au/WWWVLPages/IndonPages/WWWVL-Indonesia.html

VIDEOS/CDS

Discover Indonesia. Smithsonian Folkways. Released 2000.

Music For The Gods: The Fahnestock South Sea Expedition, Indonesia. Rykodisc. Released 1994.

Wild Indonesia. PBS Video. Released 1999.

BIBLIOGRAPHY

Indonesia. Hong Kong: APA Publications, 1992.

Atmowiloto, A. *Indonesia from the Air*. Singapore: Times Editions, 1986.

Dalton, Bill. *Indonesia Handbook*. California: Moon Publications, 1988.

Smith, Jr., and Datus C. *The Land and People of Indonesia*. New York: Lippincott, 1983.

Zach, Paul, and Edleson, Mary Jane, *Jakarta, Times Travel Library*. Singapore: Times Editions, 1987.

INDEX